"Harvey and Rathbone have struck a marvelous balance of compassionate understanding, clear and useful explanation, keen advice, and practical exercises in this valuable resource. Parents will find it a thoughtful companion to the challenging and important journey of raising their teens and young adults with emotional intensity."

—**Elizabeth Ahmann, ScD, RN, ACC**, ADHD and executive functioning coach, and section editor of "Family Matters," *Pediatric Nursing*

"Harvey and Rathbone write with a clear voice that is exceptionally instructive while never losing its caring and compassionate tone. Essential dialectical behavior therapy (DBT) skills and guiding philosophies are presented with depth and readability that emphasize mindful and effective parenting that extends into self-care and addressing the needs of siblings and extended family. Seamlessly integrating validation and practical skills and guidance, the authors light the pathways to parenting more emotionally and behaviorally balanced adolescents. This book is a superb addition to DBT and a must-read for parents with teens (and younger children) who struggle with emotions and behaviors, as well as for the therapists—DBT or otherwise—who help these families."

—**Lane Pederson, PsyD, LP, DBTC**, international DBT trainer and author of *Dialectical Behavior Therapy*

"This book is a must-read for any parent of a teen or young adult with intense emotions. The information discussed and recommendations presented are easy to follow, nonjudgmental, supportive, and effective. Readers will no longer feel that they are the only ones living in their current situations. I highly recommend it."

—**Jeanine A. Penzo, LICSW**, coauthor of *Parenting a Child Who Has Intense Emotions*, and mother of a young adult child with intense emotions and mental illness

"When your teen experiences emotions that lead to unhealthy and unsafe behaviors, it is a natural parent response to feel worried, fearful, and even angry. Often parents take their teen for help with a professional and feel unequipped to manage the emotional intensity at home. In *Parenting a Teen Who Has Intense Emotions*, Pat Harvey and Britt Rathbone offer a road map for responding effectively even in the midst of the most difficult-to-manage situations. They help parents understand the underpinnings of adolescent emotionality, describe thoughtful skills for parents to intervene and respond effectively while managing their own emotions, and offer approaches for coping with specific sets of problem behaviors. At a time when the focus for parents can feel all about their teen, Harvey and Rathbone teach parents ways to also take care of themselves and other family members. This book is a valuable and critical companion for parents in navigating the emotionally intense lives of their teenagers."

—**Julie Baron, LCSW-C**, clinical social worker and coauthor of *What Works with Teens*

"Many teens and young adults struggle to find their way through lives filled with intense emotions. They often engage in frustrating or even scary behaviors as a way to cope. Parents are looking for a way to understand these emotions and behaviors, validation about what they are going through, and concrete parenting strategies they can try with their teens. This book will be a great source of comfort and hope to many of those parents, who are doing their very best to maintain a balanced and safe life for themselves and their families in the face of ongoing crisis."

—**Elizabeth Fessenden, MA, LMHC**, director of dialectical behavior therapy services at The Bridge of Central Massachusetts, Inc.

"This book is a must-read for any parent of a teen or young adult who has intense emotions. Parents who feel emotionally battered because they've been told everything is their fault will feel tremendously relieved when they find out this is a myth that has been replaced with new scientific evidence. As readers regain their self-worth and a sense of their own importance, they'll believe it's okay to consider their own needs, too, because they must replenish themselves to keep on giving. This book belongs prominently on every parent's bookshelf."

—**Randi Kreger**, author of *The Essential Family Guide to Borderline Personality Disorder*, and coauthor of *Stop Walking on Eggshells* and two other books

"This book is immediately reassuring to parents of challenging teens and troubled young adults. It belongs in every pediatric office in the United States. The authors help parents have hope, get beyond their anger and fear, and use effective skills to deal with their child's intense emotions. Practicing the skills will help parents transform their relationships and access their love for their children while assisting them in making wise decisions in response to difficult situations. We wish we'd had this reference by our side from the beginning, and it's very helpful to us now with our young adults."

—**Eat, Study, Practice DBT Group**, Maryland

"*Parenting a Teen Who Has Intense Emotions* is a wonderful resource for parents who want to make positive changes in their relationship with their kids. It offers sound advice and clear steps to put into action right away. The simple act of validating my son's emotional state makes a big difference at those times when he is upset."

—**Kathryn Klvana**, parent of a sixteen-year-old

"This book is for every parent who yearns for a better relationship with their teen and more effective strategies to help their struggling child. We interpreted our fourteen-year-old daughter's severe emotionality as misbehavior and we locked horns repeatedly. The first time I used the dialectical behavior therapy (DBT) skill of validation and validated her distress, my daughter visibly calmed. We were able to communicate and problem solve in an entirely new way. The DBT skills have helped me be supportive, yet able to maintain effective boundaries and limits. The book offers explicit strategies for how to respond in frightening situations where you and your child are out of control. As a former teacher, I love the way the skills are laid out—simple, practical, and affirming, with familiar case studies and thoughtful pros and cons that help me think through my response. We parents are seeking to establish priorities and appropriate consequences in a world where our parental roles are not as clear as they once were. This book addresses complex conflicts with practical guidelines that will help you get past your anger to help your child and your family."

> —**Susan O, MA**, parent of a twenty-two-year-old

"This book will help you slow down and be in the moment. It will help you find some peace where you once felt constant turmoil."

> —**Lynn,** parent of a young adult who has strong emotions

"I'm in a dialectical behavior therapy (DBT) study group for parents, and we've read many books over the past three-plus years. This one is by far the most accessible guide to skills for parents of people with intense emotions. I found the chapter about siblings especially helpful, and I look forward to reading the whole book again and again as I continue to practice what I'm learning."

> —**Cindy A.**, surrounded by people who have intense emotions, including a young adult child

Parenting a Teen Who Has Intense Emotions

DBT Skills to Help Your Teen Navigate Emotional & Behavioral Challenges

PAT HARVEY, ACSW, LCSW-C
BRITT H. RATHBONE, MSSW, LCSW-C

New Harbinger Publications, Inc.

Publisher's Note

This publication is designed to provide accurate and authoritative information in regard to the subject matter covered. It is sold with the understanding that the publisher is not engaged in rendering psychological, financial, legal, or other professional services. If expert assistance or counseling is needed, the services of a competent professional should be sought.

Distributed in Canada by Raincoast Books

Copyright © 2015 by Pat Harvey and Britt H. Rathbone
New Harbinger Publications, Inc.
5674 Shattuck Avenue
Oakland, CA 94609
www.newharbinger.com

Cover design by Amy Shoup
Acquired by Tesilya Hanauer
Edited by Jean Blomquist

Library of Congress Cataloging-in-Publication Data

Harvey, Pat, author.
  Parenting a teen who has intense emotions : DBT skills to help your teen navigate emotional and behavioral challenges / Pat Harvey and Britt H. Rathbone.
    pages cm
  Includes bibliographical references.
  ISBN 978-1-62625-188-5 (pbk. : alk. paper) -- ISBN 978-1-62625-189-2 (pdf e-book) -- ISBN 978-1-62625-190-8 (epub) 1. Emotional problems of teenagers. 2. Behavior disorders in adolescence. 3. Dialectical behavior therapy. 4. Behavior disorders in adolescence--Treatment. 5. Adolescent psychotherapy--Parent participation. 6. Parenting. I. Rathbone, Britt H., author. II. Title.
  BF723.E598H373 2015
  649'.154--dc23

                                2015028416

Printed in the United States of America

20   19   18

10   9   8   7   6   5   4

To Brad, whose wisdom, support, and balance was invaluable in parenting our two teens as they grow into wonderful adults.

To all the parents of teens and young adults who are doing the best they can while also having the courage to learn how to parent ever more effectively. This book is for you, to validate your struggle and offer you hope.

—PSH

To the young people who have intense emotions. You bravely bring passion and change to our world. Although this book is written for your parents, I dedicate it to you.

—BHR

Contents

Acknowledgments

I will always be grateful to The Bridge of Central Massachusetts, the agency that provided me with my initial training in DBT. I thank Christy (Clark) Matta for teaching me the foundations, skills, and essence of DBT; she started me on this amazing DBT journey. I am also grateful to Steve Murphy, who developed the "story of emotion" and who first encouraged me to write about my work with parents.

I am continually grateful to Britt, my colleague, coauthor, and, at times, copresenter; his support, respect, and ongoing encouragement to do the most effective work we can has helped me to continue to learn and grow. I appreciate his passion for his work, which is contagious to everyone around him.

I am incredibly grateful to Jeanine Penzo, my friend, who trusted me with her thoughts and feelings, and, in sharing with me, helped me to understand the internal lives of parents whose kids have intense emotions and set me on my current professional path.

I appreciate the opportunity given to me by Britt and by Brian Corrado, another colleague, to facilitate parents DBT skills groups that paralleled the adolescent DBT skills groups in their practices. Thanks for giving me the opportunity, for a couple of years, to help you develop the parent component of your comprehensive programs while doing what I love to do.

I owe special gratitude to all the parents who trust me with their stories and who remain my greatest teachers. Their ongoing courage, willingness to learn, and ability to change always impress and excite me.

It has been such a joy to continue to work with, learn from, and experience the ongoing professional growth of my Tuesday morning consultation team—Jean Lauderback, Wyneshia Hicks, Mark Becker, Betty Bae, and Sara Jane Walker. You all are incredible professionals, and I continue to learn so much from you while I always enjoy, and receive much validation from, the time we spend together. I also appreciate the amazing professionals who were on my Rathbone consultation team—JoJo Gaul, Julie Baron, Phyllis Pomerantz, and Ben Pleasure—for the support and guidance they provided during the time we worked together.

I remain appreciative of the love and support of some very special friends who enrich my life. And, finally, words cannot express how much I appreciate my family and the meaning they bring to my life. I deeply appreciate my own children, Jenn and Sarah, amazing adults who I am so proud of and whose lives have immeasurably enriched mine; I am very grateful that you and your husbands, Neil and Brady, allow me to share in and experience the pleasure of your wonderful journeys through adulthood, continuing to teach me along the way while I also practice some of what I teach others. I am grateful for my amazing grandchildren, Josh and Molly. You add such pleasure and joy to my life. You are the most incredible distractions and remind me always to be fully present and to appreciate the wonder of life. Finally, I am always and forever grateful to my husband, Brad. Your love, unwavering support, patience, pride, and belief in me have enabled me to be the best I can be and to accomplish what I have. My family brings the balance to my life that makes all things possible.

—*Pat Harvey*

Given that this is a parenting book, and that I learn best from personal experience, I want to acknowledge my own parents. I wasn't always an easy adolescent to parent, and my parents showed tremendous patience and wisdom. My mother, Claudia, taught me assertiveness; my stepfather, Stan, taught me acceptance and validation; and my father, Bryce, taught me to accept reality. These weren't easy lessons, and I didn't always realize I was learning them. Thank you. My wife, Susan, who helped me see the world beyond my own, has given me thirty years of love and friendship, and has allowed me the flexibility to work, write, and teach. Thank you. My daughter, Huntly, continues to teach me humility and that parenting can be improved. Thank you.

I have been very lucky to work with talented and effective colleagues, and I am so grateful for all of my DBT teammates: JoJo Gaul (who was instrumental in getting DBT up and running in our setting), John Dunn, Phyllis Pomerantz, Julie Baron, Ben Pleasure, Betty Bae, Jeannette Bjorklund, and Laurie Nelson. Thank you all.

I am very thankful for my professional relationship and friendship with Pat Harvey, who tirelessly advocates for the needs of parents who are raising challenging kids. Parents need more Pats, and I'm lucky to have her in my professional and personal life. Thank you, Pat.

—*Britt Rathbone*

We are both deeply grateful to Tesilya Hanauer and New Harbinger Publications for enabling us to respond to parent requests for help with their adolescents through the publication of this book. As always, we are grateful to Jess Beebe and her team for helping us to develop a clear and well-written book. And thank you to our copy editor, Jean Blomquist, who helped us make this book more readable and accessible to parents.

—*PSH and BHR*

Introduction

As you pick up this book, are you thinking about your teen and the emotional upheaval going on in your home? Are you wondering if your teen has intense emotions and if that's the reason you experience so much disruption in your relationship and your home? Are you feeling overwhelmed by your teen's emotions and by your own reactions? Do you wish that you could find some guidance for how to manage your teen's emotions and behaviors—and yours—in a way that doesn't leave you feeling depleted, guilty, or hopeless?

We have written this book to answer your questions and to guide you with concrete, effective, and proven strategies to help you parent more effectively and to bring some order to the chaos in your life. As a therapist who specializes in working with parents (Pat) and a therapist who specializes in working with teens who have intense emotions (Britt), we wanted to write this book to provide you with guidance, support, and understanding for the challenges you face as a parent—as well as ways to understand your teen and thus parent more skillfully. We have written this book to let you know that your feelings—and your teen's—make sense given the circumstances of your life, and to provide you with hope that both your life and that of your teen can get better.

If you're the parent of a teen or young adult who has intense emotions, you may feel despair, hopelessness, helplessness, fear, worry, frustration, guilt, anger, and a myriad of other emotions. While you might feel that nobody can understand your life experience or your feelings, *you are not alone*. Many other parents share your experience, even if they do so in different ways. From our work with parents and teens in homes where there is emotional intensity, we have seen many parents who share your concerns, worries, and doubts—parents who also have been able to use the skills and strategies that we will discuss later in the book to become more effective and hopeful.

In order to use these skills and strategies, it's important first to understand your teen's experience at this time of his life. If you're living with an adolescent—a child whose chronological age spans from preteen (10–12) through the teen years (13–19) and into young adulthood (20–25)—you're well aware of the numerous changes going on in your child's life and the effect these changes have on yours. (Note: While our focus in this book will be mainly on teens, much of the information we offer also applies to preteens and young adults.) Teen bodies and brains change in dramatic and life-altering ways, which leads to an intensity of emotions that either may be entirely new to you or an exaggeration of emotions you have previously seen. As teens struggle with these changes, emotions may run high. As a parent, you struggle with these changes, too. *You may not recognize this new person living in your home and you may wonder how you can parent him in the midst of so much change and so much emotion.*

It may help to understand that as teens move toward adulthood, their task is to develop their own identity, which means they will need to separate from their parents—from you—by challenging you or even rebelling. Emotions intensify as the teen who used to respond to your limits, expectations, and moral values now challenges—and even rejects—much of what you've been teaching. You may not be ready to let go of your parenting role or authority, and you may find it difficult to accept your new, lesser role in your child's life. You're well aware of the emotional upheaval in your teen and how it affects the whole family.

If children have always been highly sensitive to emotional experiences and have been challenged emotionally and behaviorally through childhood, this emotional intensity may lead to more disruptive, and even dangerous, behaviors when they enter adolescence. Or perhaps, for example, your daughter has always been able to manage her emotions, and now, in adolescence, sadness becomes depression, anger becomes rage, and fear becomes overwhelming anxiety. As she tries to manage emotions that feel overwhelmingly painful, she may use behaviors—such as self-harm, aggression, substance abuse, disordered eating, refusing to attend school, or risky social behaviors—that significantly affect her life (and yours).

So how do you deal with your teen's experience and emotions—and your own? Dialectical behavior therapy provides some helpful guidance and direction.

Psychologist Marsha Linehan (1993a) developed dialectical behavior therapy (DBT) to help people whose intense emotions lead to self-harming and suicidal behaviors learn how to live the life they want to have. DBT concepts, skills, and strategies rest on a basic foundational concept: people need to be accepted in order to change, and both acceptance and change are necessary. In DBT, there is recognition that people are doing the best they can in this moment, given the circumstances and difficulties of their lives, *and* that they have to make changes so that they can live a life that is fulfilling to them. DBT teaches skills and strategies to help people replace dangerous and disruptive behaviors with healthier and more adaptive behaviors, all the while acknowledging how difficult it is to change.

We've taught these DBT foundational concepts, skills, and strategies, which are explained in this book, to both parents and adolescents for over a decade. They can provide you support and guidance whether or not your teen is in DBT or any structured treatment; they can help you recognize and accept your own feelings, understand and accept your teen and his experiences, and make changes so that you can parent in more balanced and effective ways. Parents who have learned and practiced these skills report positive changes in themselves, in their parenting, and in their relationships with their teens and young adults.

We've written this book with an attitude of acceptance; it's not about fault and blaming. It's based on the understanding that you are and—despite your feelings to the contrary—have been doing the best you can to parent your teen under difficult and painful circumstances. You also continue, as you read this book and utilize other resources, to search for even better ways to parent. It is our experience that these concepts and strategies provide both a means for *change* and *hope* that your life, and that of your teen or young adult, can be different and less disrupted by emotionally driven behaviors. We recognize the courage and strength it takes to read this book, to seek out ways to help your teen, and to be willing to learn and change; we hope this book will enable you to appreciate yourself and your efforts while it provides concrete guidance for making these changes happen.

What This Book Offers You

This book is divided into three parts, each of which will provide you with explanations, examples, and exercises to help you practice what you're learning. Part 1 (chapters 1–4)—Understanding Teens and Effective Parenting Strategies—provides the foundational concepts, strategies, and skills that will help you (1) to understand and accept your teen and her emotional reactions; (2) to parent more wisely by understanding, accepting, and managing your own emotional reactions to your teen; and (3) to parent more effectively by weighing the consequences of your responses to your teen, developing priorities for your decisions and choices, and strategically responding in order to increase your teen's use of safe and healthy behaviors to replace less adaptive behaviors. Part 2 (chapters 5–8)—Responding to Problem Behaviors—provides information about specific behavioral problems that result from your teen's intense emotions as well as concrete guidance about how to respond in the safest and most effective way to these behaviors, using the skills outlined in part 1. At the beginning of each chapter, you'll find a list of the behaviors that are included in the discussion in that chapter so that you can quickly find the chapter most relevant to the behavioral problems you are experiencing. Part 3 (chapters 9–10)—Caring for Self and Family—acknowledges the ways in which your teen's behaviors affect you and the rest of your family and helps you develop ways to take care of yourself, respond to the needs of your other children, and explain your teen's problems to other family members. The goal throughout the book is to provide you with support and acceptance and the ways to create change.

How to Use This Book

We recommend that you start by reading part 1 so that you understand the concepts and skills that we'll discuss in part 2. If you're feeling overwhelmed by your own emotions or the effect your teen is having on you or the rest of your family, you can read part 3 at any time. It may provide you with the support and skills you need to calm your own emotions, feel better about yourself, and feel more in control of your life so that you can more effectively implement the skills offered throughout the book. You can then pick the chapters in part 2 that are most relevant to the problems you're experiencing with your teen.

If you're already learning DBT skills in another setting, this book will provide a companion to your learning experience, a concise summary of the skills and concepts—and ways to implement them—that will enhance what you are learning. If DBT is new to you, this book will provide clear explanations and practices that will enable you to implement the skills almost immediately. Our experience is that parents can learn and utilize these skills whether or not their teen is in DBT treatment, other treatments, or no treatment.

You and your teen *can* change—and life *can* get better. The wonder of DBT is that it can transform the life of anyone who learns it. That has been our experience, and we hope it will be yours as well.

Part 1

Understanding Teens and Effective Parenting Strategies

Chapter 1

Teens, Emotions, and Behaviors

Adolescence is a time of great transition for teens and their parents. The child who was so connected to you now seems so far away. All of a sudden the peer group is of utmost importance and you feel pushed aside. At times, you may not recognize the "stranger in your midst." The child you knew has disappeared into a new body with new needs, expectations, goals, behaviors, and, yes, heightened emotions. For some parents, their teen is an exaggeration of the child they knew: a quiet child now appears more sullen and isolated; a more outgoing child may become more assertive, independent, and less willing to accept limits. For other parents, the changes may be more dramatic; a once cooperative and seemingly happy child may become less compliant or more depressed, or a quieter child may have more friends and be more outgoing. And you, the parent, may find yourself trying to understand this new person while at the same time missing the child you knew. As your child transitions and changes, so must you and your parenting.

Adolescence is also a time of great change for teens. Changes in their brains allow them to see and understand in new ways. Their emerging ability to think more abstractly leads to more insight into differences and choices. They (1) often reject their parents in order to find themselves, (2) can be at once confused and emboldened by their changing bodies and their developing cognitive abilities, (3) seek others who feel the same way and try to become just like them so that they have an anchor in an otherwise shaky existence, and (4) provide few cues, or sometimes contradictory cues, to their parents as to what they need or what they want. Their confusion becomes yours. Your teen may reject any connection to you at one moment ("Please, Mom, drop me off down the block from school") and seek your absolute attention at the next moment when it may be less convenient for you ("I know it's late, Dad; I just have to talk to you now"). You may spend a great deal of time wondering how to respond, how to be helpful, and how to maintain your own sanity and your own life in the midst of these ongoing, shifting demands and expectations.

Some children may have always seemed to be emotionally intense or sensitive, reacting immediately and strongly to situations that other kids seem to just ignore. How does adolescence affect your child if she has already experienced emotional challenges like depression, anxiety, or angry explosions? And how do you manage your own emotions and your emotional responses to your child? How do you handle your fears for your child, your concerns about her future, your everyday conflict?

Whether your child experiences intense emotions or the typical emotional conflicts and mood swings of adolescence, her emotions are quite real, and cannot and should not be dismissed or otherwise trivialized. Though these emotions are often exasperating for parents (and for the teen as well), they impact behaviors and decisions. Those emotions may also be the driving force behind the behaviors that create problems for you and/or your teen. Understanding emotions, where they come from, and how they develop will help your teen or young adult manage them safely and effectively. You will also personally benefit from understanding emotions; your awareness of your own emotions will help you respond more effectively to your teen or young adult. This chapter will help you understand adolescence, emotions, and the connection between emotions and behaviors so that you can apply this understanding to the skills discussed throughout this book.

Adolescence: A Time of Challenge, Change, and Unpredictability

The world of the adolescent is complicated and filled with challenge, change, and unpredictability. Contributing to the confusion is the fact that adolescence begins and ends at different times for everyone. The onset of puberty—a typical signal for the start of adolescence—occurs between fourth and tenth grade for most young people. Visit any middle school and this variation is on full display. The effect of hormonal changes on emotionality is well understood and exacerbates expression of feelings for those who may already be predisposed to emotional intensity. On the other end of development, there is no clear and evident indicator for the end of adolescence. If we consider that adolescence is the bridge between childhood and adulthood, and if we define adulthood as independence, financial and otherwise, then adolescence extends well into the third decade of life for many young people, and parents remain a significant part of the lives of adolescents, be they preteens, teens, or young adults.

Temperament

Every child is born with a unique, biologically based personality, or *temperament*, that is evident in a variety of settings and remains fairly consistent over time. You may notice that the temperament of one of your children is very different from another's, and you may wonder how this can be. You probably noticed these traits in early childhood, and these may be the same challenging traits that you face during adolescence. Below we discuss several ways that temperament is related to how emotions are experienced. As you read through these different traits, consider how your own temperament interacts with that of your child.

Strong and Powerful Emotions

One aspect of temperament is how strongly people experience their emotions. Some children have very intense emotional experiences, and others seem to feel their emotions more mildly. Teens with less powerful and intense emotions are generally less challenging for parents. On the other hand, young people who deeply and powerfully experience feelings display passion that can have a significant influence on others. At the same time, their lows may be very hard and have a bigger effect on their behavior. Parents can get worn out by this ongoing intensity and may underreact as their children reach adolescence. They can become immune to these intense emotional reactions of their teens. Other parents will match their teen's mood intensity with their own, which usually results in increased yelling and conflict. Temperament traits are inherited to some degree, and often parents have similar intensity, which allows for greater empathy on the one hand and, at the same time, can result in escalating expression of emotions.

Initial Reaction to New Situations

Some children tend to jump immediately into new situations, while others are slower to engage and will observe from the sidelines before doing something new. Some kids make friends easily, while others are more anxious in social situations. Both of these styles pose challenges for parents. If your teen is eager to try new activities without much orientation, she may be at risk for acting impulsively, and is at risk for a host of behaviors that might worry you (substance use, reckless driving, risky sexual behavior, and so on). If your teen is more cautious, you may worry that she appears isolated and doesn't initiate or take part in new activities. You may worry less about dangerous consequences and more about the limited life your teen seems to be living.

Sensitivity to Sensations

Some young people find themselves reacting sensitively to their environment. They may be particular about their clothes, avoiding certain fabrics that are rough or itchy, or they may be irritated by tags in their clothes. Or they may be bothered by bright or flickering lights, loud noises, and/or smells. You may struggle to understand your teen if she reacts this sensitively to the environment, especially if you're not aware of the biological origins of these responses. If you have similar traits, you'll usually find it easier to empathize with and comfort your teen.

Adapting to Change

Change, even positive change, can be hard to get used to. Consider the energy expended getting used to a new job or new relationship. And consider the amount of change that young people experience routinely through their adolescence, including new schools, body changes, and social disruptions. Some teens find it very easy to adapt to these changes, which in turn makes it easier for parents. Teens who adjust more slowly to the changes and transitions in their lives often find adolescence more difficult and are typically more challenging for parents, who struggle to provide ongoing helpful reassurance and support.

Brain Development

Adding complexity to parenting your teen is the impact of her developing brain. The decade from ages ten to twenty, perhaps longer, is a time of explosive brain development. In short, the areas of the brain responsible for logical and strategic responses are "under construction," while the emotional centers of the brain are active and seemingly unrestrained. This is familiar to parents who routinely witness their teen children reacting with emotional outbursts and responses that seem irrational or illogical. While this biological process of brain development is not within the control of the teen, it does make living with a teen, especially one with intense emotions, feel incredibly difficult to her parents.

Nature and Nurture

Your child's temperament interacts with yours from her earliest days. She may smile and coo at you from early on, or she may cry regardless of how much you try to comfort her. Parents often note that the way they parent one child does not work for other children. You know how competent you might feel parenting the child who responds so well to your touch and your voice, and you might feel inadequate or frustrated if your child doesn't smile at you or cries regardless of what you do. Your child teaches you through her behaviors what does and doesn't work. She also affects how you'll feel about yourself as a parent. So you, as a parent, are as much a product of your child's interactions with you as your child is a product of your interactions with her. This is a *transactional model*; you and your child influence and change each other based on your own temperaments and how you respond to each other.

Biosocial Theory

Some teens experience ongoing intense and at times overwhelming emotions that may be painful and very difficult for them to manage. They may develop a pervasive difficulty in regulating emotions, which leads to increased difficulty handling emotional situations. This *emotion dysregulation* underlies many problematic behaviors that we will discuss in the second part of this book. The *biosocial theory* of emotion dysregulation (Linehan 1993a) explains how pervasive emotion dysregulation develops; it is a transactional model and does not blame parents or the teen for the problems that develop.

Emotion Dysregulation

Some children are born with a brain that is more emotionally sensitive than other children. The child reacts immediately and intensely to situations that others might not notice or respond to. It may seem to you that your child has gone from 0 to 100 on the emotional scale in a matter of seconds and, once at that high level of emotion, has a very slow return to her more typical emotional level. This child is unable to manage these emotions and therefore learns, through experience, ways to avoid or escape them.

Invalidating Environment

Most parents, upon seeing this intense emotional reaction to a seemingly (to them) minor issue, will be confused and upset themselves. When confronted by your child's painful emotions, you'll try to find ways to help her feel better, sometimes by inadvertently trivializing or dismissing her emotions. When you are not aware of your child's emotional sensitivity, you may (1) attempt to help her get over her feelings by saying things like "It's really nothing" or "Just forget about it"; (2) try to comfort or reassure her with statements like "It's okay," "Don't worry about it," or "Tomorrow will be a better day"; or (3) try to fix the situation or give advice by saying something like "Did you talk to your teacher about that problem?" or "Next time, why don't you do it this way?" For many children, these statements may help them feel better and move on. For your child who has emotional intensity, these statements may actually serve to "invalidate" how she feels, making it seem as though her feelings don't matter or do not make sense.

The impact of the invalidating environment. A child who feels her emotions intensely will become quite confused when the environment (parents, teachers, friends, and so on) around her dismisses, trivializes, or questions what she's feeling. This response invalidates the child's experience. She will begin to wonder why she feels awful when others say it isn't a big deal or what is wrong with her that she feels something that others tell her not to feel. This child may begin to question her own very real emotional experiences. Then she may either express emotions even more loudly to ensure that others know how much distress she's in, or she may begin to hide her emotions from others, denying them, even to herself, until she eventually explodes in ways that take everyone by surprise. Some teens go back and forth between dramatically expressing their emotions and trying to hide them; either way, they create ongoing problems for themselves and their parents.

Teens whose emotions are dismissed, even inadvertently, do not then learn effective skills to manage them. Teens who have been invalidated do not learn they can tolerate and live with painful emotions, and they try to find ways to diminish the pain they feel, often using dangerous or unsafe means.

The Impact of the Biosocial Theory on Parents and Teens

When this theory is explained to parents and to teens (either individually or together), the relief can be felt by all. The teen begins to realize that how she feels is not the result of a personality flaw. She realizes that her brain functions differently from other members of her family and that this isn't her fault or a problem in and of itself. You, her parent, might also find that you now have an explanation for what has seemed inexplicable and frightening for many years. You're not blamed; you can be comforted with a new knowledge base that makes sense. This theory of nature *and* nurture then provides the basis for many of the skills discussed in this book that will help you respond in a more validating, less dismissive, and more effective manner.

The Story of Emotion

How do emotions develop? Where do they come from? How can you understand why sometimes your teen goes from being upset to screaming, punching a wall, or harming herself when at other times she goes quietly to her room? Why are you able, sometimes, to show understanding and support to your teen and accept her behaviors when, at other times, the same behavior might cause you to get angry and yell? Emotional experiences don't just happen. They develop through a series of steps that eventually link thoughts, feelings, and behaviors. Understanding how thoughts affect feelings, which then influence behaviors, will provide you with ways to change your emotions and the behaviors that result from them. The *story of emotion* explains how feelings develop and how we act as a result. We will look at these steps in more detail now.

Vulnerability Factors for Parents and Teens

Vulnerability factors are those situations or feelings that contribute to how we will respond to situations or events as they arise. When you're vulnerable, you tend to react more intensely and negatively to situations. Some vulnerability factors are fatigue, hunger, illness, lack of exercise, being out of your usual routine, visiting places or people who have caused stress in the past, or not doing enough things in your life that bring you pleasure or feelings of competence. You might also be vulnerable when routines are disrupted by situations or events, even if these are generally happy events, such as a wedding or family reunion. Any of these situations might make it harder to manage emotional reactions to events as they arise.

Teens have all the same vulnerability factors as adults. In addition, they may have vulnerability factors related to the issues of adolescence: impact of hormones, real or imagined peer problems, feelings of isolation, worries about school and academic performance, uncertainty about their own identity, their own disappointments or their fears that they are disappointing their parents (despite any statement from the parents to the contrary). Some teens are able to respond easily to changes in schedules or disruptions to their expectations. For other teens, any transition or change in routine is difficult to manage.

The Prompting Events

The *prompting events* are the situations, events, thoughts, or feelings that prompt the chain that leads to the emotional experience. You're probably aware of situations that tend to upset your teen, such as being told no, a limit being enforced, being teased by a sibling, a friend getting angry, or a teacher asking more of her than she thinks she can handle. You're probably also aware of things your teen says or does that upset you. It's impossible for you or your teen to avoid all prompting events, and in actuality, you both need to learn how to manage these situations. When you're aware that your teen has reacted emotionally to a prompting event, you can be sensitive, helpful, and supportive while helping your teen to navigate her emotions and the situation. And when you react emotionally to a prompting event, you have to help yourself similarly.

Thoughts

Thoughts are the statements we make to ourselves that express what we believe or how we interpret the prompting event. These thoughts tend to include judgments about what happened or might happen and are usually so automatic that we are not even aware of them. For example, you might react to your teen's tone with anger without being aware that you had the thought *She should not speak so disrespectfully to me.* Thoughts might reflect the belief systems we were raised with, the expectations we have of ourselves and others, or our moral compass. The more awareness we have of what we're thinking, the more we can change those thoughts and ultimately change how we feel.

Your teen has a set of beliefs and self-statements that have an effect on how a prompting event will make her feel. Teens can be filled with self-doubt (despite behaviors that seem to indicate the contrary), and thoughts like *I am so stupid* or *I am such a loser—why can't I do what others can?* may be internal responses to any criticism (or perceived criticism) no matter how minor it might seem to the parent. The social world of the teen can be harsh and critical, and teens may adopt highly critical self-assessment in social situations. Teens also have strong feelings and expectations; their responses to a prompting event might be based on what they think "should" or "is supposed" to happen in certain situations. For example, teens might get angry at parents who remind them to do their chores because they are thinking, without realizing it, *Why do they keep bothering me? I should be in charge of myself and what I do.* Sometimes a teen's rigid thinking might make it hard to accept situations that she cannot change, which might lead to frustration or despair.

You are often not privy to the internal struggles of your teen or young adult, which can leave you feeling helpless and confused. In the next two chapters, we will provide you with ways to respond to your teen, even if you're not sure exactly what she's thinking or feeling.

Body Sensations

Body sensations are the way your body feels when you're having thoughts that generate feelings. You may notice butterflies in your stomach, a headache, tension across your forehead, tension in your shoulders or back, clammy hands, or difficulty breathing, or you may be aware that your heart is racing. All of these body sensations are signals of an emotional reaction. Be aware of what your body is telling you so you can respond to these sensations in ways that may reduce or lessen the intensity of your emotions. (We will discuss this further in chapter 3.)

Teens' bodies are already in a state of flux, and they may be confused by the array of body sensations they're feeling. This makes it even harder for them to identify the physiological responses that signal an emotion. They may have to be taught how emotions feel in their body so that they can be aware of these emotional signals.

Give Your Emotion a Name

It is useful to name your emotion so that you can communicate it to yourself and others. Those butterflies in your stomach may be signaling that you're anxious; the sense of being tired may signal depression or sadness. Some people (teenagers often among them) can identify only a few emotions; they may know only that they feel upset or angry. They may not recognize or accept emotions such as jealousy, disappointment, pride, frustration, or even joy, satisfaction, and elation. And yet we all have a range of emotions, all of which are important, and which serve a function and signal that there is something that we need to respond to. When you identify your emotions by name, you more easily communicate what you're feeling to yourself and to others.

Behaviors

Some people think that the story ends with the emotion. And yet it's not the emotion that causes concern or difficulties; it's the action or way the emotion is expressed that is usually the problem. A teen may sit in her room feeling very angry, and while this may be a difficult situation for her, it does not cause problems unless she begins to behave in a dangerous or unsafe way. While emotions often lead to urges to act in a certain way, you and your teen can make effective choices about what behavior or action will be used to express an emotion. These actions can lead to feeling okay at the end of the story or may lead to more problems and more stories.

● A Teen's Story of Emotion

Karen is a sixteen-year-old sophomore in high school. She has a learning disability that has made learning and schoolwork more difficult for her, although she's working hard to keep up with her classes. Her english class has been particularly difficult, and she has been having trouble completing her assignments for that class. She has been staying up late at night to try to get her work done, and she continues to be frustrated by her inability to complete her assignments. Her parents, for whom schoolwork is very important, are frustrated and angry when they become aware that some homework assignments have not been handed in. They try to talk to Karen about this while she's doing her work, and she explodes in anger and blames them for all the problems she's having. She tells them that they just don't understand, demands that they leave her alone, and refuses to speak to them for the rest of the day. Her parents remain angry at her. She is so distracted and upset by the situation that she doesn't complete her work.

Karen's story of emotion might look like this:

Vulnerability Factors

Karen is already feeling stressed by how hard it is for her to learn in general. She may also be overwhelmed and frustrated that she's not able to complete the assignments in her class. She's also tired from staying up late at night.

Prompting Event

Karen's parents are frustrated by her not completing her assignments and try to talk to her about this. Talking to her while she's working is the prompting event for Karen.

Thoughts or Beliefs About This Event

Karen thinks, Why can't they get me? I hate that they're blaming me for something that isn't my fault. Why can't they trust me and just leave me alone? I hate them.

Emotion Names

Karen is angry and frustrated.

Actions/Expression of Emotion

Karen begins to yell at her parents, blames them, and then refuses to speak with them. She doesn't complete her assignment, which makes her feel even worse.

Aftereffects

Karen may feel guilt and shame about her behavior and frustration with her inability to complete her assignment. While her internal feelings may remain hidden from those around her, they may continue to affect how she feels and how she continues to behave for some time after this event ends for her parents. It might even be the vulnerability factor or the prompting event for another story of emotion.

Changing the Outcome of the Story

How might this story have had a different outcome? The story of emotion provides a blueprint for the development of emotions as well as the guidance for how to change the outcome of the story and the way you, or your teen, might feel after the emotion is expressed behaviorally. It also shows the ways that the story of the parent transacts with the story of the teen (with each story affecting the other back and forth), providing ongoing opportunities to respond differently. As a parent, it helps to be aware of your own story—your own vulnerabilities, prompting events, thoughts and interpretations, body sensations, and actions—as well as those of your teen. Your action may be your teen's prompting event and vice versa. Your teen's vulnerability factors might trigger yours or may be your own prompting event and vice versa. Changing one story will often change the other.

Vulnerability Factors

When you're aware that your teen is vulnerable, consider the effect of your behaviors; be more sensitive to monitoring your own behaviors, reactions, or expectations of your teen during those times. It might be helpful to avoid confrontations or increasing demands. Being aware of vulnerabilities—yours and your teen's—allows you to choose the most effective time to discuss situations with her. Awareness of vulnerability factors may help you to minimize anger and frustration within the family.

> When Karen's parents are aware that Karen is tired and already stressed, they might decide to let her continue to do her work and try to find a time when she's more relaxed to have this discussion with her. Or, when they recognize their own frustrations and vulnerabilities, they may decide that Karen was already trying to do the best she could and perhaps not approach this topic at all. When Karen is aware of her vulnerabilities, she might be able to tell her parents that this discussion might cause her to lose her concentration and that she's not prepared to have the discussion at that time. When both parents and kids are aware of vulnerabilities, the rest of the story might be entirely different.

Thoughts and Feelings About the Event

The way we think affects the way we feel. Thoughts are changeable. That means that thoughts can be changed, which changes feelings as well.

Karen's story might be different when she's able to think, *My parents are trying to be helpful to me even though they may be annoying and irritating me. Maybe if I tell them I'm working on the assignment, they'll go away and I'll be able to concentrate on my work.* Karen's parents will find it easier to manage their own emotions when they keep in mind that Karen's behaviors might be a result of her learning disabilities instead of lack of motivation or willingness.

Body Sensations

When you're aware of how you're feeling in your body, even if you're not sure why, you can find ways to soothe yourself and calm down your body sensations. We will discuss ways that you can manage your body sensations in chapter 3. Your teen can also develop awareness of her body sensations and find ways that she can soothe herself. Karen's parents or a professional counselor might help Karen learn that taking a moment to relax her body can ultimately change how she feels.

When Karen notices that her neck is feeling tense, she might get up and stretch or even ask her parents if she could go out and take a walk or play with their dog. When she's aware that her fists are balled up, she can open them up and stretch her fingers or use lotion on her hands. Any of those actions will help her feel calmer and lessen the intensity of her emotions.

Behavior

It might seem that our actions or behaviors are out of our control. This is not actually the case. While each emotion causes people to want to act in a certain way (what is called an *action urge*), often you and your teen can choose how to express the emotion and use another behavior in place of the initial urge to act in a way that would not be productive.

Karen may have remembered that, despite her anger at her parents, it usually worked better for her if she calmly asked them to leave her room and let her work rather than yelling at them, which usually made her feel worse and made it harder to concentrate. She then would not have felt as bad about herself (or her parents) and might have been able to concentrate on her assignment. At the same time, her parents may have realized that they needed to let Karen do her work without interruption, and they may have held their comments to her for a later time.

Primary and Secondary Emotions

Prompting events lead to thoughts and emotions, which influence each other. This initial feeling to a situation is the *primary emotion*. Primary emotions are immediate reactions to situations (for example, you're happy when you achieve, you're afraid when you're attacked). There are also times when the primary emotion itself, and how we think about it, becomes a prompting event for another, *secondary emotion*, or feelings about feelings.

The way in which you react to your feelings is affected by your belief systems about emotions, by how you may have been brought up to think about emotions, and by your own expectations of yourself. If you believe that "parents should not get angry at their kids," then you may feel guilty when you do get angry. If you expect that "I should be very understanding of the issues that my teen faces," then you may be frustrated when you get angry at or frustrated with her. These are secondary emotions.

In Karen's story, her parents may begin to think, *We should be more understanding and less frustrated. We know it's hard for her and that she's trying.* Or Karen might think, *I shouldn't have gotten so angry at my parents.* These thoughts by either Karen or her parents might lead to another emotion, such as guilt.

We create our own secondary emotions. While your primary emotion might last only seconds, the secondary emotion may last much longer and may become a "mood" when you continue to think about it and judge yourself. Being aware of your secondary emotions provides one more way to gain control over your emotions and behaviors. Secondary emotions can also lead to their own behaviors; if you feel guilty about how you treated your teen, you might try to "make it up to her" by doing things for her that her behavior doesn't warrant, and that isn't helpful in the long run. Or a teen's secondary emotion might lead to an escalation of anger and additional problematic behaviors.

In Karen's story, her parents don't know the shame and guilt she feels after she explodes at them. They don't know that her own belief that she should be able to manage her emotions better leaves her feeling ashamed of herself. Teens often feel shame about their behavior; and yet, because shame is such a difficult emotion to experience, they try to blame others and deflect their own feelings. Parents may assume, often erroneously, that their teen "doesn't care" about how she behaves; this is rarely the case. If you understand and accept that your teen may have significant secondary emotions, it might help you become less angry and frustrated and more understanding, even if you still don't like the behavior.

Understanding the Function of Behaviors

The story of emotion illustrates how emotions lead to behaviors. You may wonder why your teen chooses to respond to painful emotions with dangerous, unsafe, or aggressive behavior. While it might not be clear to you, the behaviors of your teen serve a purpose—that is, the behaviors help her in some way to regulate emotions and reduce pain. To understand this further, we can look at Reva's story and then assess the pros and cons of the behavior she chooses to help manage her emotions.

Reva is an eighteen-year-old senior who has had difficulty making friends throughout high school. She has always been anxious and worries about what her peers think about her. This leads her to isolate herself and be withdrawn and quiet when she's with others. Often she's depressed and lonely and wants very much for her life to be different. She complains to her parents that she just wants to feel better and be able to have friends without all the anxiety she feels whenever she's around her peer group.

In the past six months, unbeknownst to her parents, Reva has been going into their liquor cabinet and drinking their wine and vodka. She finds she is calmer and less worried when she drinks. She has also found that when she goes out with other kids and has a drink before she leaves, she's less inhibited in her actions and feels better. Her peer group approves of her behaviors because she's so much fun to be around and continues to ask her to join them, which helps her feel less depressed. She continues to drink because it feels so good and she feels so much better.

Eventually, her grades begin to slip as she cannot concentrate or focus the way she used to. She's also more tired and is sometimes unable to get up to go to school. Her parents begin to get frustrated with her school attendance and performance and begin to limit her outside activities. They also begin to watch her more carefully, which leads them to find out about the drinking. They decide to take away her car and other privileges as punishment for her behavior.

In order to understand why a teen behaves the ways she does and to understand the function of her behavioral choices, it's helpful to look at the pros and cons of the behavior that the teen uses as well as the pros and cons of healthier, safer behaviors (Linehan 1993b). This helps you understand why a teen might continue to act in a way that has negative consequences. Using Reva's situation as an example, we can look at how she would perceive the positive and negative consequences of continuing to drink and the pros and cons of staying sober.

Drinking

Positive Consequences

- feel better, calmer immediately

- feel more relaxed

- able to be with friends

- feel less lonely, less anxious

- get along with peers without worrying so much

Negative Consequences

- school attendance drops

- lower grades

- unable to concentrate on work

- parents get angry

- lose privileges

- tired more often

Not Drinking/Staying Sober

Positive Consequences

- able to concentrate

- get to school more often

- better grades

- get along with parents

- have more freedom and more privileges

Negative Consequences

- continue to experience anxiety and depression

- not able to be as comfortable with peers

- more isolating

- not feeling as calm or relaxed

It becomes clear that drinking provides Reva with immediate relief from her discomfort (which is the goal of the behavior), while the negative consequences, such as lower grades or difficulties with parents, are future issues that may not be as important to her. While adults might also seek immediate relief, teens (whose brains are not yet fully developed) are often not able to think about long-term consequences when what they want is an immediate way to manage painful feelings. You also might notice what is not always clear to others—that sobriety has its own negative consequences; Reva has to feel the uncomfortable feelings she's seeking to escape from.

From looking at the positive and negative consequences of their teen's behaviors, parents can learn several things:

- A dangerous or unsafe behavior may have a function and serve a purpose. Those behaviors reduce the teen's emotional pain.

- There are reasons why a teen would engage in behaviors that seem inexplicable to the adults in her life.

- Healthy behaviors may have a downside in that the teen may have to experience the discomfort or pain she's seeking to avoid.

- The pros of a dangerous behavior are immediate, while the cons are longer term.

- The pros of a safe behavior are longer term, while the cons are immediate.

Summary

In this chapter, we provided you with an understanding of adolescence, how temperament affects the way teens perceive and respond to their world, and the way in which a teen might develop intense emotions. We also discussed emotions and how emotions might lead to particular behaviors.

Key Points:

- Adolescence is a time in which your child's brain develops and changes, while she also tries to separate from you and develop her own identity.

- Emotion dysregulation—that is, pervasive distress and the intense behaviors that result—develops when a brain that is wired to react intensely is met by an environment that may dismiss or trivialize the reaction, even if inadvertently.

- An emotion is affected by the way a person *thinks about* an event.

- People can choose behaviors that will communicate their emotion.

- Behaviors that may be problematic in the long term frequently help teens lessen their painful emotions in the short term.

Chapter 2

Effective Parenting

Like other parents, you may often question yourself about your role when raising your teen: What should I attend to? What's important and what's not? You may be confused when a response from you is met with cooperation one day and anger the next. You might try to find ways to connect, while your teen wants distance. Your teen's confusion becomes your own. You and your teen differ in what you think and feel, and you often have a hard time accepting and understanding each other.

If your teen experiences intense emotions that are hard for her to manage skillfully (see chapter 1), the problems are intensified and you may find that strategies that have worked with your other kids are not effective with this one. The confusion you experience is exacerbated by your fear when your teen acts in dangerous or unsafe ways. You may have learned through prior experience not to set limits or have expectations and to respond in ways your teen wants in order to avoid potentially dangerous or threatening reactions. You, like other parents in similar situations, may experience exhaustion, distress, and despair as you try to raise a child responsibly while also trying to keep him, and your home, safe and calm.

Effective parenting means doing what works to accomplish your goals, both in the short run and the long run. It's not necessarily what might be fair or what you think "should" work, based on your past experiences or beliefs. It means looking at a situation, assessing your priorities, and determining what responses will help you achieve your goals at this time and in these circumstances. Effective parenting requires you to (1) remain calm in the midst of your teen's emotional outbursts, (2) understand and acknowledge your teen in the context of his life and experiences, and (3) implement strategies that will enable you to de-escalate situations, prioritize what you will respond to, and respond to your teen or young adult with insight and understanding. These are interrelated; you will have a hard time implementing these new strategies if you do not remain calm. We discuss how to remain calm and how to respond with new insights in this chapter. We discuss specific strategies in chapter 3.

States of Mind

Recognizing states of mind, in which emotions may dominate at times and logic and rational thinking may dominate at other times, helps you respond to your teen with more balance. Effective parenting uses this recognition to synthesize emotional experiencing and reasonable thinking; this synthesis enables wise decision making (Linehan 1993b). On one end of the spectrum, some people respond to the world and make decisions and choices based on their "gut"—how they feel influences what they think. On the other end of the spectrum, some respond in a very rational, measured way, thinking about what is logical and sequential without considering emotions at all. Thinking wisely takes into consideration both emotion and reason and leads to decisions that tend to be more intuitive and effective.

Reacting in an Emotional State of Mind

You're probably aware of when your teen is in an emotional state of mind. Yelling, screaming, doors slamming, accusations, and abusive language or threats are all reliable signals. Or your teen may totally shut down. When your teen reacts emotionally, he is, much to your dismay and frustration, not able to hear what you believe are reasonable comments or explanations. This is because emotional intensity often interferes with logical thinking.

You are also probably aware of those times—when you feel you have a "short fuse" or want to scream or cry—when you react in an emotional state of mind. Despite your desire not to, you may react emotionally to your teen's intense emotions, getting caught in that adolescent emotional vortex. Your emotions, too, interfere with your ability to think clearly, plan, or problem-solve. When you're aware that you're reacting in an emotional way, you can take steps to move toward a calmer, wiser, more effective way of responding.

Explaining in a Rational State of Mind

A teen or a parent who acts, plans, or makes decisions in a purely rational frame of mind is thinking about logic and facts, and does not take into consideration the effect of emotions on situations and decisions. If you function mostly in a logical way, you may not understand why someone else reacts emotionally. It just doesn't make sense to you.

Adolescence is a time of heightened emotionality, and parents rarely see the teen who makes plans without experiencing the impact of emotions. Perhaps you frequently try to reason with your teen who is reacting emotionally. When you find yourself lecturing your teen or showing him newspaper or magazine articles to prove your point, you are probably in a rational state of mind. As you talk, your teen probably ignores or becomes annoyed with you, and nothing productive actually happens.

Responding in a Wise State of Mind

Parenting effectively means finding the wisest responses to situations—that is, those responses that integrate both emotion and reason and consider long-term goals. A decision made in a wise state of mind is intuitive, takes into account the whole picture, and feels, on a deep level, like the most effective thing to do. A teen who decides he needs to attend therapy or go to study sessions after school despite a desire to be out with his friends is making decisions in a wise state of mind. A teen who knows he has to attend a family celebration even if his friends think this is a "stupid" way to spend an evening is also in a wise state of mind.

You are most likely in a wise state of mind when you (1) recognize that your teen is reacting emotionally, (2) stand back and not lecture, (3) listen to what your teen is saying and not judge, (4) remain calm and acknowledge your teen's point of view, and (5) respond in a way that will help you achieve your goals. Parents who acknowledge the emotional turmoil or dangerous behaviors of their teen and access professional help in any way may do so with ambivalence and some emotional difficulty, while also knowing it's the "right thing" to do. You are probably in a wise state of mind when you make decisions that may be painful and difficult *and* that, at the same time, you know are necessary.

Developing Wise Responses by Being Mindful

How does a parent find wise responses, especially when interactions with teens (whether or not they have intense emotions) are often so emotionally charged? Parents often become emotionally reactive to their teen due to past events, concerns about the future, and/or their own internal experiences (being tired, hungry, not feeling well, and so on) that may be unrelated to the teen. Developing wise responses requires "mindfulness." *Being mindful* means focusing on the present moment without judgment, and it allows you to respond deliberately in ways that integrate emotion and reason and that are effective in the moment (Linehan 1993b).

There are a number of things you can do to help minimize your own emotionality. Responding wisely does not mean that you push aside your own emotions; it means that you take active steps to notice and accept your own thoughts and emotions so that you can manage them effectively. Then you can assess the situation clearly and implement the wisest and most effective response.

Slow Down

The first and most helpful thing you can do to lessen your emotional reactivity is to slow down. There are a variety of ways to accomplish this:

- Take a deep breath to clear your thinking.

- Remind yourself to make decisions with your coparent and not rush into responding to your teen, even if he's demanding an immediate response.

- Remind yourself that your teen is doing the best he can in that moment.

- Take a time-out or even retreat to the bathroom to buy some time to think clearly and effectively.

Parents tell us that when they slow down, they are able to think more clearly and understand their teen's point of view. They are then able to follow through in ways that will eventually lead them to a wise state of mind and the ability to respond effectively to their teen.

Parent Practice: Slowing Down

Set a timer for two minutes and do the following:

Focus on printing your name very slowly on a piece of paper. Notice that you will have to think about what you're doing more than usual. Notice what it feels like to write in ways that are different from what you generally and automatically do. Notice the sensations in your hand as you write. Notice how your name looks different when you print it slowly.

By slowing down and paying attention to the sensations associated with something as automatic as writing your name, you recognize that you can slow down and make changes in many other behaviors.

Notice Your Situation and Surroundings

To notice means developing an experiential awareness of your situation and surroundings without using words. It can be very hard to do this. To understand this more, think about a young child who doesn't yet talk. If you watch the child, you can see him exploring his world, and he may not have the words yet to describe it. The young child learns through physical exploration and so can you.

When you notice, you become aware of things that you hadn't been aware of before. How often do you walk down the street without noticing what surrounds you? You don't see, for example, a new flower bed until you actively work on becoming aware of what's around you. It is this way in families as well; you may not notice patterns that exist within your family until you take the time to slow down and notice. And it is only when you notice something that you can take active steps to change it.

Parent Practice: Noticing

Pick up something that's familiar to you, like your keys or wallet. Notice how it feels when you touch it. Turn it over; look at it from different angles. Just feel; do not use words. Do you notice anything new?

Focus on the Moment with Your Full Attention

Giving your full attention to what you're doing in this moment is a powerful skill that helps parents respond wisely. Distracting thoughts about the past or future make it much harder to respond effectively in the present. It can be challenging to stay fully engaged on one thing in the present moment when you constantly face so many demands. While you might feel like you need to multitask, this actually results in being less effective in all the tasks. Being fully present and focused on one thing leads to effective behaviors.

Parent Practice: Focus on the Moment

Pick a routine behavior (such as loading the dishwasher, eating, driving) that you do automatically. Focus on the task with your full attention, without multitasking, and when your mind wanders, bring it back to the behavior.

Describe Without Judgment

Once you notice something, you may then want to use words to describe it. It's most effective to describe in ways that replicate what you're actually seeing so that someone else can "see" what you're describing as it exists or happens, without interpretation. The words you use both reflect and influence the way you think, which affects the way you feel and, ultimately, the way you act. One way that you can learn to react less emotionally and respond more wisely is to speak and think in nonjudgmental terms, using words that don't judge. Think about how you *feel* when you describe your teen, even to yourself, as "manipulative" or "attention seeking." You may become angry, frustrated, or disappointed. Now think about how you *feel* when you think that your teen does whatever is necessary to get his needs met, and he is resourceful in getting others to pay attention to him. You might feel less angry and maybe even proud of him.

Parents sometimes erroneously think that using nonjudgmental language means that you use more positive language. Actually, using nonjudgmental language is about describing and not using judgments, labels, or evaluations of any kind. Nonjudgmental feedback, however, can include preferences and opinions. For example, you might say, "Everyone seemed to enjoy themselves when you were telling stories at the dinner table tonight. When you spend time with us the way you did tonight, I really enjoy your company." This provides information about your expectations. If, however, you say that your teen "behaves well," even though the language is positive, it tells him little and might make him feel like you're judging him. Nonjudgmental feedback provides information without judgments of any kind.

When you think and speak in a nonjudgmental way, you do not assume the intent or reason for a behavior. You might think that you know what your teen wants or doesn't want, when you're actually making assumptions or interpreting behavior. If you say, "My teen doesn't want to do his work" or "My son doesn't care about school," these assumptions feel like facts to you and might lead you to have negative feelings. And yet you don't really know your teen's thoughts, feelings, intentions, motivations, or desires. What you *know*—which is what you observe and therefore can describe—is that he's playing video games and not doing his work. You don't know, and won't always accurately assume, the reason. Nor can you assume the intent of a behavior by its consequence. Though a behavior may *result* in your being mad, that doesn't mean that your teen's *intent* was to make you mad. Assumptions, treated as facts, may lead to conclusions and responses that are emotionally driven, off the mark, unhelpful, and not effective. There is usually more to the story than what's evident. It helps you respond more wisely and effectively when you describe behaviors that you see and don't make assumptions about what cannot be seen.

It's hard to start thinking in a nonjudgmental way. Everyone learns to use shortcuts to label people and behaviors and to communicate. The problem is that these words often evoke emotions, and they increase your emotional reactivity. You'll realize, as you begin to think nonjudgmentally, that you feel differently toward your teen and that you respond with less emotionality.

In the left column of the following chart is a list of commonly used labels and judgmental terms. The right column offers descriptions of the same behaviors in ways that do not evaluate or judge.

Judgmental Labels/Descriptions	Nonjudgmental Descriptions
• He always seeks attention.	• He acts in ways that cause others to attend to him.
• He's lazy.	• He doesn't get up and do the things we ask.
• He's unmotivated.	• He doesn't complete tasks.
• He's manipulative.	• He does whatever he can to get his needs met. If he doesn't get the answer he wants, he asks someone else.
• He's out of control.	• He screams and yells and throws things when he doesn't get what he wants.
• He doesn't want to get better.	• He isn't using the skills he's learned.

Parent Practice: Describe Without Judgment

Think about a time when you felt angry, disappointed, or frustrated with your teen. Notice any judgmental thoughts, assumptions, or words like "should," "shouldn't," "must," or "appropriate." Next, try to describe the behaviors that you actually observed, without making assumptions or labeling. Write down your nonjudgmental description of your teen's behaviors on a piece of paper or in a journal.

Do What Works

People ultimately want to act and respond in ways that help them achieve their goals. And yet people continue to repeat behaviors that haven't worked in the past. They do this because these behaviors are familiar and comfortable, albeit ineffective, and because change is very hard. Remember that it's as hard for you to change as it is for your teen. Ask yourself if what you're doing is getting you closer to your goal. If not, you may want to change the behavior. When you slow down, pay attention, and think in nonjudgmental ways, it's easier to come up with a plan that will work and is more likely to get you where you want to be. These behaviors are the keys to effective parenting.

Parent Practice: Do What Works

Imagine a situation in which your teen has refused to do something you asked or is demanding something you don't want to give him. How do you usually react to these situations? Write down your initial behavioral reaction to your teen in this situation. Now, think about your goals, what you want to accomplish—for example, keeping the calm in the house, getting your teen to do what is asked. Then write down a response that might be more effective.

Assumptions About Your Teen...and You

DBT puts forward a number of assumptions that create an accepting and understanding perspective about people who have intense emotions. Parents can also use these assumptions to become less emotionally reactive and judgmental and more effective and understanding of their teens (Miller, Rathus, and Linehan 2007).

Your Teen Is Doing the Best He Can at This Moment…and So Are You

It's sometimes really hard to believe that your teen is doing the best he can. He may do his schoolwork at times and then not do it at other times. You may find that sometimes he's talkative and shares what's going on in his life, and other times he withdraws to his room and doesn't talk to you at all. Your teen may be self-harming, using substances, or behaving in other unhealthy ways. You may ask how you can assume that this is the best he can do.

Everyone has good days and not-so-good days. You may go to work on a day that you're tired or not feeling well and do the best you can, knowing that this is not the same "best" that you've done at other times. Circumstances, and how you feel, can affect what your best is at any moment. Likewise, your teen's abilities will change based on how he feels physically and emotionally. His behaviors are "mood dependent," just like most people's, and how he acts is very much related to his emotional state at any moment and the difficulties he faces in his life.

Likewise, you're also doing the best you can under difficult circumstances. If you're parenting a teen or young adult who has intense emotions, every day may be filled with chaos, pain, fear, or uncertainty. You may question yourself on a daily basis as well as revisit all the decisions and everything that you have done up until now. You *have* done the best you could to raise your child with the knowledge you had, your own history of being parented, and your life experience. The fact that you may have made mistakes does not negate that you did the best you could.

This assumption may be difficult for you to accept, as it is for many parents. You may see your teen struggling at times and behaving more effectively at other times. You may not want to believe that this is the best he can do. It might help you to think that it's the best he can do *at this moment* and that there can still be hope for change in the future. It might help you to practice this statement by saying it to yourself at difficult times: *He's doing the best he can at this moment.* It serves as both a reminder and a way to calm yourself so you can respond more effectively.

If your teen is struggling, self-harming, or involved in dangerous behaviors, this may be the best he can do at this moment in time. He also has to change so that he can have the life he wants, which brings us to the second assumption.

Your Teen Needs to Change in Order to Have the Life He Wants...and So Do You

Effective parenting blends acceptance *and* change. You can accept that your teen is doing the best he can at this moment and also continue to expect him to make changes in his behaviors and in his life. The previous assumption helps to lessen your reactivity, and this one validates your belief that change is necessary. Your teen learns that he needs to change how he reacts and behaves so that he can have the life he wants. And you are reading this book because you recognize that you have to make some changes in your responses and decisions to parent more effectively and increase the likelihood that your teen will make the changes that he needs to make.

Together these two assumptions comprise the dialectic of acceptance *and* change (Linehan 1993a, 1993b); despite what appear to be contradictory ideas, both are valid and necessary. You and your teen are doing the best you can *and* you both need to make changes so that your lives can be closer to what you would like them to be. We will talk more about the concept of dialectics in chapter 4.

Your Teen Wants to Make Improvements in His Life and His Life Is Unsatisfactory As It Is Currently Being Lived

Some parents believe that their teen is quite happy with his life, despite the fact that he may fail in school or have no friends. They may see a teen who is isolated in his room with his computer and believe that he's content. He may even verbally confirm this. And yet most teens really want more than this. What teen wants to fail in school? It helps to accept that your teen is not satisfied with his life, despite evidence to the contrary, and that he wants to make his life better despite all the difficulties he's having. It may not be clear what's getting in his way, although he most likely does desire to have a better life. Remembering this helps you feel less angry, disappointed, and frustrated.

It's often easier for parents to be angry and frustrated than it is to be sad about their teen's life. Acknowledging that your teen is not happy with his life helps you to feel *his* pain, while it also may make you feel sadness that he's suffering. This is a natural response to these assumptions. When your anger gives way to sadness and compassion, it helps you become more understanding and more supportive of your teen and enables you to be less reactive and more effective.

Your Teen May Not Have Caused His Problems and Only He Can Change Them

Teens often blame their parents or others for their problems and think they're the ones who have to do the changing. Parents may think it's their responsibility to fix their teen and may be frustrated in their attempts to get their teen help that he may not take advantage of. The reality is that, despite where the problems come from, a teen is the only one who can change himself. Parents (or therapists, for that matter) may provide the opportunities for change and still not be able to change teens no matter how hard they try, if the teen himself is not doing the work he needs to do to change.

You may have a hard time with this assumption, believing that your child is your responsibility and it's up to you to help (or fix) him. As hard as it is, many parents are relieved when they are able to adopt this assumption, finally being able to feel somewhat free of the incredible, and ultimately impossible, expectation that they can change someone else, even if that person is their child. This assumption might help you, even as the reality frustrates you, accept that you can provide access to the best services for your teen, make the changes to parent more effectively, make necessary changes in the environment, *and* still your teen is the only one who can make the changes necessary to have the life he wants to have.

Teens ultimately learn that blaming others doesn't change the reality of their lives or the fact that they have to work to make changes in their behaviors if they want their lives to be different. Teens are often not ready to do this work at the same time that parents think they need to be making changes. You may have to accept that change will be up to your teen, and, while you're doing the best you can, you cannot help someone who is not ready to accept and utilize the help that is offered.

Your Teen Needs to Learn Behaviors in All Areas of Life

Most parents have had the experience of watching their teen, who may be sullen and angry at home, become social and cooperative with his friends. Parents may go to school and not recognize the uncooperative teen who is described by his teachers. Behaviors in teens are mood dependent, so it's not unusual for them to behave differently in different environments. Differences in behaviors do not mean that a teen is "choosing" to behave calmer, safer, or more effectively in some environments than in others; it means that he feels differently and then acts differently. Your teen will need to learn how to use calmer and safer behaviors in *all* environments that he encounters, regardless of how he feels in each, so that his behavior is more consistent and his life as a whole can be better.

There Is Validity in Different Points of View

Parents and teens often see situations quite differently. Your natural inclination may be to argue with your teen when he claims that you "never let me do anything," pointing out all the examples that make him wrong even as he's doing the same to prove *his* point. Each of you is trying to prove that your truth is the *real* truth. And it's hard to "agree to disagree" or walk away when you feel like your teen's truth is so far from what *you* think is reality. People sometimes spend a great deal of time trying, unsuccessfully, to convince others that "I'm right and you're wrong."

It becomes apparent very quickly that arguing over whose "truth" is the "real truth" will only lead to an increase in frustration and anger. If your goal is to lessen emotionality and verbal sparring, engaging in this power struggle is not effective. What can you do in this situation to be effective? Recognize that you may not be able to change someone else's mind, even if that someone else is your own teen. Accept that there does not have to be a right or wrong, only what will be effective in meeting your goal—*and* continue to set your limit. Your teen does not have to agree, and you do not have to prove that you're right. State your expectations and do not get sidetracked by the discussion of who is right or wrong. Stay focused on the issue at hand and accept that there can be different points of view.

Parent Practice: Using Assumptions to Parent Effectively

Write your answers to these questions on a piece of paper or in a journal:

- Which assumption will help you the most? Why?

- Which assumption is the hardest for you to accept? Why? How can you work on accepting it?

- Think about a situation in which you had an emotional reaction to your teen. Which assumption might help you respond more wisely?

Validation: Communicating Understanding and Acceptance

Validation is the way you let your teen know that you "get it," that you understand what he's saying or feeling given his experiences and the context of *his* life (Linehan 1993a). It does not mean that you agree with him, approve of, or like what he's saying. Validation lets your teen know that you're taking him seriously, acknowledges what he's saying without judgment, and lets him know that you're trying to understand from his perspective. In parent-teen interactions, validation is one of the most important and helpful skills you can learn and practice. Validation promotes healthier families, leads to more self-disclosure, and calms down emotional situations (Fruzzetti 2005). By developing a validating environment, you lessen the impact of your teen's biologically based emotional vulnerability. Parents report a difference in their interactions with their teens, a decrease in emotionality, and an ability to communicate better almost immediately when they begin to validate.

For every interaction in which your teen has said, "You don't get me" or "You're clueless," validation is the antidote. Invalidation leads to anger and frustration; validation has the potential to lead to understanding and calmer interactions. Adolescents want their parents to get what they're going through, how they feel, and why they're doing what they're doing. This is the challenge for parents. Here are some examples of statements your teen might make and what his underlying feelings might be:

- When your teen says, "My problems are your fault," he might be thinking, *I'm so ashamed and feel so badly about the ways I act sometimes.*

- When your teen says, "You're the worst parent ever," he might be thinking, *I'm really angry and frustrated about the way you treat me.*

- When your teen says, "You never let me do anything I want to do," he might be thinking, *I feel left out when I can't do the same things as my friends.*

- When your teen says, "Leave me alone. I hate you," he might be thinking, *I really wish you understood me and how hard things are for me.*

When you recognize, accept, and acknowledge the thoughts and feelings behind the words, you can validate more effectively. While this is a skill that you will need to practice over and over again, you will find, as many other parents have, that it leads to more positive interactions, more sharing from your teen, and fewer incidents of escalated emotions.

How to Validate

Parents often want to fix their kid's problems or soothe his feelings in an effort to help him feel better. Responses like "Don't worry about it," "You'll feel better tomorrow," or "Just calm down" may be sincerely offered as ways to diminish your teen's emotions and yet may have the opposite effect. Your teen might actually get angrier because he isn't feeling heard. Likewise, an attempt to dismiss your teen's self-judgments or thoughts ("You aren't a loser, sweetheart"), even if you're trying to help him feel better about himself, may be experienced as invalidating. If your teen feels terrible about himself, relate to his feeling ("You must be feeling pretty awful"), not to the specifics of his words.

Emotionality gets in the way of validation (Fruzzetti 2005). You have to be calm in order to effectively validate your teen. This is especially difficult if your teen's anger or frustration is aimed at you. Parents often ask how to validate a teen who's yelling directly at them and saying very hurtful things. You can start by genuinely acknowledging that he's angry with you, even if you disagree with what he's saying. It helps to accept that he wants you to understand what he's feeling, even if he's not clearly stating what those feelings are. When you are calmer, you will see, and then validate effectively, what is behind the actual words.

Validation must be genuine to be effective. Teens, especially those who are emotionally sensitive, know when you're not being honest and will sometimes not accept your words. Don't say something that you don't believe; search for what you do accept as valid, such as your teen's feelings, how a situation feels to him, or what his life might feel like. Remember that validation doesn't mean that you agree; it simply communicates your understanding that the way he feels and behaves makes sense given all the complexities of his temperament, experiences, and the current situation.

Validation is idiosyncratic. What will work for each teen will vary, and trial and error leads to what soothes *your* teen and helps him feel heard and understood. Let him know you're trying to get it, even if you might have missed the mark. If your teen dismisses your attempt at validation, try again. Validation is in the ear of the receiver, so ask your teen what he finds helpful. The effort will not go unnoticed, even if he doesn't acknowledge it. We provide some guidelines and examples of validating statements on the next page.

Validation: Guidelines and Examples

Guidelines for Validation

- Stop, listen, observe: slow down your response, notice your emotions or judgments, and respond wisely, not emotionally.

- Ask questions.

- Try to understand the behavior in terms of your teen's life.

- Look at what your teen might be feeling or experiencing.

- Respond to the feelings, not to the words: reflect back the emotion without judgments ("You are really angry/upset/frustrated right now").

- Experiment with different forms of validation and see what works: (1) Listen with focused attention (without necessarily saying anything), make eye contact, and stay focused in the moment. (2) Repeat back—in your own words—the gist of what your teen is saying. (3) Acknowledge that you can understand his behavior based on his past experiences and/or a sense of what others might feel in a similar situation.

- Be mindful of your own nonverbal signals, tone, or body language, which can be validating or invalidating without you actually realizing it.

- Try not to offer advice or fix a problem, unless you have been asked first.

Examples of Validation

- "Please tell me more."

- "Wow, that sounds like a really difficult situation."

- "I see why you're feeling that way. Is there some way that I can help you feel better?"

- "I see that you're angry/sad/frustrated/disappointed."

- "Other kids would probably feel like that if it happened to them."

- "I'd feel like that too, if that happened to me."

Look for What's Valid

Jared is a fourteen-year-old ninth grader who recently has been experiencing increasing difficulties with his anger and frustration toward his parents. Jared also seemed unhappy if his friends didn't do what he wanted them to do, and he didn't cooperate when they asked him to do something. His parents have heard him yelling obscenities at his friends and are beginning to notice that his friends are coming over less often, and Jared is staying home more. One day Jared complains to his parents that his friends didn't invite him to a party and he's very upset. He appears sad.

Parents who are faced with situations like this might have a number of different responses, each one trying to help their son in some way. Do any of these statements sound familiar?

- "This party isn't such a big deal. We're sure you'll be invited to lots of other parties in the future" (*minimizing his feelings*).

- "Let's go do something fun together so you don't have to think about the party" (*dismissing his feelings and trying to make him feel better by distracting him*).

- "We've seen how you've been treating your friends and understand why they wouldn't want you at the party. You should try being nicer and not yelling at them, if you want to be invited in the future" (*blaming and reasoning with him when he's emotional*).

After any of the above responses, Jared might feel that his parents didn't understand how unfair this felt to him and how upset he was, even though they were trying to be helpful. He might feel dismissed, which might increase, rather than lessen, his anger and sadness. If his parents minimize his painful feelings and try to distract him with other activities, he might learn that painful emotions can just be forgotten and he won't learn from the experience. Or he might be angry that his parents were suggesting that this situation was his fault when he saw it differently. With these responses, he would not feel understood and would not accept the need for more skillful behaviors.

This is a situation in which validation is necessary. Jared's parents will be effective by acknowledging the sadness and anger that he's most likely experiencing and genuinely reflecting this back to him. They might say, "I would be upset too, if I wasn't invited to a party" or "Anyone would feel angry in this situation." It is only after this validation, and a lessening of his emotional intensity, that Jared will be able to listen when his parents talk to him about how his behaviors might have contributed to this situation. This is the power of effectively balancing acceptance and change.

To better understand how Jared's parents can validate effectively, consider how one parent might have experienced this situation, thought about it, and responded.

Description of the situation:

My son told me he's upset because his friends are having a party and haven't invited him. I've seen him yelling at his friends lately. My son says he's angry about this and appears sad.

My thoughts and feelings about this situation are:

I think my son has to take some responsibility for his behaviors and recognize that he has somehow created this situation. Maybe if he learns how to treat his friends better, he'll also treat me better, which would be nice. I know how his friends feel, and yet I feel sorry for him and don't want to see him sad.

What I can understand my teen is experiencing is:

He's very angry, and possibly embarrassed, that he hasn't been invited to a party. He may not truly know or be able to face his role in losing his friends. He may be worried about how he'll be viewed by others if he doesn't attend the party that his friends attend.

I can acknowledge that I'm hearing and understanding my teen in the context of his life by saying:

I'm sorry you didn't get invited to the party. I know you must be angry and disappointed. I would feel bad, too, if I wasn't invited to a party my friends were going to.

Next steps:

My son heard what I said and didn't get angrier. Later we were able to talk calmly about some of his recent behaviors and how he's feeling these days, and figure out how he might handle things differently so that he would be able to reengage with his friends.

Parent Practice: Validating Your Teen

You can practice validating your teen by completing the sentences below on a separate sheet of paper or in a journal:

- This is a nonjudgmental description of a situation I'm facing with my teen…

- My thoughts and feelings about this situation are…

- When I think about the situation nonjudgmentally, I realize what my teen is experiencing is…

- This is the way that I can let my teen know that I'm hearing and understanding him…

- The next steps are…

Acceptance: What It Is

Adolescence, defined as a time in which kids are separating from their parents, frequently means that the young person and his parents disagree quite often. Parents who try to change the attitude or behaviors of their teen children often find themselves in conflict or power struggles. When a teen has intense emotions, the conflict might escalate into self-harming, aggressive, or otherwise unsafe or dangerous behaviors. It may be more effective (and safer) to accept that you don't have as much control over your teen's behaviors or attitudes as you did when he was younger. At the same time, you feel it's your responsibility to help your teen grow into an adult who makes safe choices and behaves in moral and healthy ways. You feel as if you're giving up and/or behaving irresponsibly if you accept behaviors, choices, or attitudes that you don't agree with.

Radical acceptance means fully and completely accepting that "it is what it is" and that often things are beyond our control (Linehan 1993b). This powerful skill helps parents reduce emotional suffering while increasing effective problem solving. Just as validation does not mean that you agree with the behavior of your teen, so acceptance is not a passive way of giving in or giving up. It is, paradoxically, a way to move forward.

The Benefits of Acceptance

It's not always easy to accept those things that you disagree with or that are not what you expected. Think of the baseball game that you had intended to go to with your whole family. Making the plans has not been easy and you're looking forward to it. Then it rains and the game is postponed. You can walk around angry and disappointed and focus all of your attention on how unfair it is that you cannot go to the ball game. Or you can accept that there is no choice in this situation; and once you accept this reality, you can make plans to spend time with the family in a different way. Not accepting leads to more suffering and to being "stuck"; acceptance allows you to move on.

If your child had emotional difficulties when he was younger, it may have taken some time for you to accept that he had additional needs. You might have tried to deny this initially, telling yourself that he was going through a phase and that he just needed to mature. Or you might have been angry at others who might have suggested that he needed additional help. Prior to accepting that your child has emotional difficulties, you did not seek out the support that he (and you) needed. Once you accept the reality of the situation, however, you are able to get help and move forward in a constructive, effective way.

Ongoing Acceptance

When a child has emotional difficulties or intense emotions, acceptance is an ongoing process. You may have to accept that your child needs support, treatment, or a special school placement. The acceptance that a child has emotional difficulties is like the grief and mourning of any loss, except it continues to happen over and over again. Your child may get better and then get worse. You may have hope that all is well and then be faced with a significant decline in your child's ability to manage his emotions safely. As difficult as it may be, you may have to accept that the child you have is not the child you expected and dreamed about. Your life and the life of your child may be more difficult than you had ever anticipated. The pain and grief of letting go of the child of your dreams and hopes will lead to the acceptance of the teen or young adult that you have. It will also lead to the ongoing process of finding the most effective supports and helping your teen have the most productive life he can. Acceptance, thus, does not mean giving up hope. It enables you to hope that the future will actually be different than the present.

Accepting Is an Active Process

Acceptance does not just happen; it is an active process that requires turning your mind toward a willingness to accept through (1) being aware of how your body feels, (2) being aware of your thoughts, and (3) relaxing your body to enable new information and new awareness to enter your consciousness. It means recognizing with your whole body and spirit that you have no choice, that reality is what it is, and then moving on to problem-solving how to make the most out of a difficult and painful reality (Linehan 1993b).

Some of the ways that you might begin to accept include speaking or writing down the reality that you're having trouble with, looking at the consequences of accepting this reality (both negative and positive), and allowing yourself to grieve for the reality that you had hoped for (Linehan 1993b). If you're feeling stuck, try to assess what you might not be accepting. Allow yourself to think about a different reality. Experience your disappointment and your anger. Then allow yourself to move forward into a new reality. You will feel better *and* parent more effectively.

Summary

This chapter focused on how you can parent effectively by learning skills to help you remain calm while also understanding and acknowledging your teen's perspective and feelings.

Key Points:

- Develop awareness by slowing down, thinking wisely, and incorporating both emotion and reason into your responses.

- Use validation to acknowledge the feelings of your teen and to let him know that you take what he's saying seriously. This will also lower the intensity in emotional situations.

- Accept your teen as he is in this moment, even as you remain hopeful for change in the future.

- Accept yourself and your efforts to be the most effective parent you can be.

Chapter 3

Parenting Strategies

If you're the parent of a teen who has intense emotions, you're probably looking for guidance on how to effectively respond to the emotional upheaval that you're experiencing. In the introduction, we discussed how skills and strategies that are taught in dialectical behavior therapy (DBT) help people manage painful emotions in safe and healthy ways (Linehan 1993a). These same skills can also help you parent effectively when your teen is overwhelmed by painful emotions and may be exhibiting dangerous or unsafe behaviors. The strategies we discuss in this chapter include skills that help you to (1) choose effective responses, (2) de-escalate dangerous situations, (3) establish priorities even when you feel overwhelmed, and (4) help your teen when she is overwhelmed by her own pain and distress.

Strategy: Considering Pros and Cons

In chapter 1, we discussed why a teen might choose to act in a particular way by looking at the positive and negative consequences of a teen's unsafe versus healthy behavior. You can use the same strategy when choosing how to respond to your teen. We can explore the pros and cons of parent choices through this vignette:

Sheila is an eighteen-year-old recent high school graduate who was hospitalized several times during high school for expressing a desire to die and threatening to kill herself. She has a history of self-harm and substance abuse related to painful emotions. She was treated by a therapist and received medication, which she stopped taking when she turned eighteen. She now refuses to attend therapy, saying that her problems are behind her and she just wants to be "normal." Her goal is to stay at home for a year, possibly take some courses locally or online, and then go away to college. Her parents have asked her to get a part-time job or do some volunteer work. Sheila spends most of her time in her room, using social media to talk to her friends and communicate with other kids who have histories similar to hers. She expects her parents to pay for her social activities and for a car that she can drive to those activities. They're angry and frustrated by her ongoing demands when she has not met any of their expectations. They're also afraid of what she'll do if they don't give her what she wants. When she asks them to buy tickets to an out-of-state concert, they initially say no. When she says that she doesn't want to live if she can't go to the concert, they become anxious and are not sure what to do. The positive and negative consequences of their choices would look like this:

Giving Her What She Wants

Positive Consequences

- She won't harm herself.

- She won't be angry at them.

- They can give her some pleasure and enjoyment.

- They can feel like they're being "nice" parents.

Negative Consequences

- She'll continue to demand things from them without meeting any expectations.

- The situation won't change, and she won't learn anything that would encourage her to change her behaviors.

- They'll remain angry and frustrated.

- She'll learn that she can get what she wants when she threatens them.

Saying No to Her Request

Positive Consequences

- She may learn to act more responsibly and meet some expectations so she can earn what she wants.

- There's a possibility for change in her behaviors at home.

- She may learn that she won't get what she wants by threatening suicide.

Negative Consequences

- She'll be angry at them.

- She may act out at them, perhaps in a dangerous way, because she's disappointed.

- They may be sad and worry about not allowing her to do something that brings her pleasure when she has so little enjoyment in her life.

- They'll be anxious that she may do something dangerous to herself like accidentally, or intentionally, kill herself.

When Sheila's parents used this list of positive and negative consequences to help them make decisions, they gained three major insights: (1) the situation won't change and their daughter won't make any changes in her behaviors if they continue to respond with the same pattern of responses to her, (2) they're anxious and afraid that she might be dangerous to herself if they say no to her, and (3) they're making decisions that work in the short term (by lessening the immediate threats) and that also have a negative long-term effect by reinforcing Sheila's belief that she can get what she wants even if she doesn't do what's expected. You might develop similar insights when you make a list of the positive and negative consequences of your choices.

If your teen has a history of suicidality or any other dangerous behavior, you may be so afraid for her safety that you continue to give in to whatever demands she makes. You then find yourself in the same situation again and again as you inadvertently reinforce threatening and unsafe behavior by giving her what she wants. Your teen has no incentive to change her behaviors. Meanwhile, your frustrations continue as she gets privileges without meeting any expectations or making any healthy changes in her life. This dilemma is quite real, quite distressing, and quite painful. While it may be understandable, repeating the same behaviors is not effective in bringing about change in the family.

Facing Risks and Making Changes

When parents look at the positive and negative consequences of their responses, they recognize that if there is to be any long-term change, they need to respond to their teen differently and accept that there may be risk involved. If they want their teen to accept some responsibility, they will have to be prepared to withhold privileges until she meets some basic expectations.

When your teen has intense emotions, you need to make these potentially risky choices and decisions after careful thought. Your teen may, in fact, react dangerously, and you have to be comfortable that you're acting in the wisest, most effective way to help her move toward a safer and healthier lifestyle. You'll need to carefully and continually weigh the short-term and long-term benefits of your choices, the risks and the possibilities. Don't feel pressured to behave in any way that would make it difficult to live with a potentially dangerous outcome. Ultimately, you have to be able to live with your decision. Be mindful and caring about yourself as you make these decisions for the future of your family.

Strategy: Understanding Emotions

Parents' emotions, like their teen's, develop through a series of steps that we earlier called the "story of emotion" (see chapter 1). A story of emotion includes vulnerability factors, prompting events, thoughts about the event, body sensations, naming the emotion, and, eventually, the behavioral response to the emotion. Often the stories of teens and their parents intersect; the teen's behavioral response can be the prompting event that triggers an emotional response for the parent, and the opposite is also often true. It's important for you to understand your own story of emotion so that you can manage your own emotions skillfully and respond most effectively to your teen. To see how this might work, we'll look at the story of Sheila's parents' emotions to see how they can make changes in their emotions and responses. Their story may provide insight into how you can make similar changes in your emotions and responses.

Vulnerability Factors

Sheila's parents are continually on edge and anxious because they never know when Sheila will become angry or suicidal or when she might self-harm. They're upset that she's not doing what they've asked her to do. They also worry about the quality of her life going forward. This leads them to feel vulnerable to negative emotions and to be more reactive when Sheila makes demands on them. It's harder for them to think wisely.

Reducing Vulnerability to Negative Emotions

You can reduce your vulnerability to negative emotions (Linehan 1993b) in several ways. You may find these approaches helpful:

1. Increase positive experiences by making sure there are pleasant activities in your life—and in your teen's life.

2. Enjoy and appreciate the moments when you're having fun with your teen or when she's behaving in healthy ways. At these times,

don't focus on when the "next shoe will drop." Be present in the current moment, acknowledge it, appreciate it, and enjoy it.

3. Make sure you—and your teen—are doing things in your life that make you feel competent and accomplished. Try not to demand more of yourself in other areas of your life that will increase your anxiety. Likewise, try to encourage your teen to do things that make her feel competent without asking for more than she's capable of doing. Experiencing accomplishments lessens vulnerabilities for parents and teens.

4. Plan in advance for situations that may cause anxiety, even if these situations are happy events. Young people who have intense emotions, and their parents, often feel emotional in different or new circumstances, such as big family events or parties or other situations that may not seem stressful for others. As you prepare for these events, talk to your teen and prepare for how to respond to the increased anxiety. Recognizing the possibility that your emotions or those of your teen may be escalated enables you to minimize them or skillfully manage them when they arise.

5. Take care of your physical health and well-being and encourage your teen to do the same. Getting enough sleep and exercise and eating well contribute to a sense of wellness and lessen your vulnerability to other stressful or emotional situations.

Prompting Events

Sheila's parents are triggered when (1) they see her staying in her room and not looking for a job, (2) she doesn't attend therapy or take her meds, and (3) she threatens to harm herself if they don't give her what she wants. The prompting event is not something that you can control or change; you can only change your response to the event through self-awareness and behavioral change.

Thoughts About the Prompting Event

We all engage in internal dialogues that we may not be aware of. You will, for example, have thoughts about prompting events that will affect how you feel about them. Sheila's parents probably think something like *Here we go again. She does nothing that we ask her to do. She's so manipulative and always has to have things her way. And what happens if she means it this time? What do we do if we say no and she actually harms herself? We won't be able to live with ourselves if she does that.*

Changing Thoughts

Changing the way we think about a situation can have a big impact on our overall experience. Rather than thinking that Sheila's behavior is manipulative, Sheila's parents could think that she is doing the best she can in this moment, which might help them take a nonjudgmental stance and become less angry and frustrated with her. They can take a nonjudgmental stance by thinking, *She's frustrated and trying to get her needs met. This doesn't mean that we have to give her privileges unless she earns them.* They can acknowledge to themselves that it's scary to set limits with a teen who's threatening self-harm and also remind themselves that giving in to her means that Sheila's behaviors will likely continue. At the same time, they want to provide as much safety as possible by being more vigilant until she's calmer.

Recognizing and Responding to Body Sensations

Sheila's parents might recognize the familiar sense of tension in their necks and faces, an increased heart rate, and butterflies in their stomachs. Soothing behaviors such as taking some quiet time for themselves, counting to ten, drinking warm tea, taking a walk, or taking a deep breath can help Sheila's parents slow down, feel somewhat calmer, and move from reacting emotionally to responding effectively.

Name the Emotion

Sheila's parents recognize their primary emotions as fear and anxiety, in addition to anger and frustration. They also feel ashamed and embarrassed that their parenting has not led to their daughter meeting developmental steps in ways they had hoped. They notice their secondary emotions of anger toward themselves and disappointment in themselves for being angry and frustrated at Sheila, even though they know she has problems.

Using Skills with the Story of Emotion

The story of emotion provides you with opportunities to use the strategies that we will present in the rest of this chapter. Each part of the story of emotion offers an opportunity to use different skills—planning ahead, thinking differently, self-soothing—so that you can respond in ways that might have a more effective short- and long-term outcome. Over time, the story of emotion will be more familiar and you will be able to use your story to know which strategies will be most helpful when, so that you can respond to your teen in the calmest and most effective way.

Parent Practice: Develop Your Story of Emotion

Think about an emotional experience that left you feeling ineffective. Use the following outline to write your story on a piece of paper or in a journal.

- Vulnerability factors: How was I feeling before the event?

- Prompting event: What situation or event led to the feelings?

- Thoughts about the event: What did I think about this?

- Body sensations: What did I feel in my body?

- Name the emotion: What word describes how I felt?

- Action: How did I act in this situation?

- Aftereffects: What were the consequences of my action?

Remember that any step in this story can have numerous responses. Each change can result in a different outcome.

Strategy: Changing Responses

The last part of the story of emotion describes the way you *respond* to your teen. Every emotion leads to an urge to act in a particular way (for example, when you're sad, you might feel like crying). You can, however, choose to behave in a different way. Sheila's parents might want to scream or yell at Sheila or continue to make demands on her, which might make them feel better in the moment and worse in the long run. They may want to escape their intense anxiety and fears by giving Sheila what she wants in order to dissipate the threat of self-harm, which will also not be effective.

Acting Opposite

Doing the opposite of what you feel like doing when you are upset (or *acting opposite*) is one way to change your response to your teen. When you are anxious and want to avoid a conversation with your teen because you fear an outburst, the opposite action would be to approach your teen and begin to talk, rather than walking away from her. Acting opposite, over time, actually lessens the intensity of the emotion and enables you to respond more effectively. Though it might not be easy, when you speak gently, your anger will lessen; when you keep yourself busy and active, you will feel less sad and depressed (Linehan 1993b).

One of the emotions that many parents experience is guilt. You may feel in some way responsible for your teen's pain and believe that you could have or should have done something different to have prevented this. One way you might respond to this guilt, without even realizing it, is to give your teen what she wants. It may help you let go of your guilt when you accept that you did nothing to deliberately harm her, and therefore, there is no reason to feel guilty. In order to parent effectively, act opposite to your urge and do not give your teen whatever she wants.

Sheila's parents may feel the urge to scream at her or to give in to her. In order to parent more effectively, they act opposite—that is, they speak in a soft voice and validate her feelings without giving her what she's demanding. They can remind her in a calm and gentle way that they'll be more willing to give her what she wants when she meets some of her responsibilities.

Strategy: Establishing Priorities

Parents whose teens have intense emotions are often faced with an abundance of dilemmas and choices about what behaviors to respond to and which to let go. You may wonder how to prioritize your expectations and limits when there are so many behaviors that seem to demand your attention. How do you respond when your teen (1) doesn't meet any expectations or responsibilities and still wants to participate in social activities, (2) may be self-harming or acting in dangerous ways and still wants unsupervised freedoms, (3) doesn't participate in school or work and wants you to pay for things she wants, (4) acts aggressively or abusively toward you and still wants you to do things for her, or (5) will not participate in treatment despite having unsafe or dangerous behaviors? You may find yourself trying to figure out which issues to prioritize, what to ignore, and how to make the most effective and safest decisions.

Prioritizing Your Responses When Your Teen Is Unsafe

If your teen is unsafe in any way, keeping her from endangering her life will be your main priority, even if your decisions make her angry or unhappy. Unsafe behaviors may include deliberate self-harm, acting in dangerous ways (drunk driving), or impulsive, risk-taking behavior that your teen may not think is unsafe (substance use when at a party with strangers, "hooking up," or meeting people she met on the Internet). Responding to these behaviors takes precedence over dealing with other behaviors, including school, work, or family relationships. Keeping your teen safe may include checking her room for substances, pills, or razors, even if this means breaching her privacy. It may also mean denying requests for freedoms, privileges, or activities if her judgment and choices in those situations puts her at risk. Even when your teen gets angry or pleads with you to let her do what "makes her happy," you'll need to stay focused on not allowing her to engage in behaviors that might endanger her life.

If your teen behaves in dangerous or unsafe ways, you'll want to help her engage in treatment so that she can learn safer ways to manage her painful and intense emotions. She may not agree that she needs any help and may tell you that she's "fine" and "not crazy." It sometimes helps to reassure her that she isn't "crazy," and that there are forms of treatment that will help her behave in ways that will result in her having the freedoms, privacy, and privileges that she wants to have. The goal would be helping her have the things she wants in her life. Try to remind her of the ways that therapy might be helpful to her when she seems to be suffering the most or bemoaning the way her life is. Keep your focus on finding opportunities to stress the importance of participating in treatment.

If your teen is in treatment, you may also need to prioritize getting her to participate actively by making sure she gets to appointments and even giving her incentives (rewards) if necessary for attending. Treatment appointments take precedence over *any* other activities (including extracurricular activities or sports) that she may want to take part in. You will need to stay firm if your teen wants to skip a treatment appointment to do something else she wants to do, even if she gets angry or tells you that you're "ruining her life." Once the teen learns, through her treatment, how to behave in a safe and healthy manner, she can have a lifetime of activities.

Prioritizing Your Responses When Your Teen Is Safe

If your teen is safe, you may want to put some emphasis on responding to the other issues that affect her life. These issues may include problems at school or work; issues with parents, friends, or partners; use of substances, sexual acting out, lack of friends, social isolation, too much computer use; or problems or difficulties that arise in her other activities.

It's often challenging to decide how to prioritize these issues. You may wonder, as many parents do, if you should allow social activities that may lighten your teen's mood even if homework or other expectations aren't met. You'll need to determine your own priorities and then make your decisions based on what you decide is most important for your teen. For example, if you want to prioritize responsibility and the importance of meeting expectations, you may decide that social activities are contingent upon completing a chore or homework. If you're concerned about your teen's depression or social withdrawal, you may allow her to spend more time with friends when she wants to than you might otherwise have allowed. You'll need to think about the values you want to teach as you make decisions about what to expect and what to allow. These very personal decisions are driven by your values and can only be made by you when you're thinking wisely, not emotionally.

It's important for you to be clear about your priorities so that you can deliver consistent messages to your teen. These priorities also provide you with guidance as you make decisions on a daily basis (or as often as necessary) by helping you to think wisely about what's in the best interest of the *long-term* emotional and physical health of your teen.

Strategy: Using Consequences Effectively

All behavior can be understood within the context in which it occurs, and all behaviors result in consequences. Consequences can be positive (increasing the likelihood that the behavior will occur again) or negative (lessening the likelihood of the behavior happening again), internal (such as feeling guilt or contentment) or external (such as losing privileges or receiving praise). Effective parenting means being aware that your responses affect the behaviors of your teen and then using your responses to increase adaptive, healthy behaviors (by strategically responding and paying attention to them) and to diminish unsafe behaviors (by strategically not responding to them).

Reinforcement and Punishment

Responses that are likely to increase the possibility that the behavior will occur again are called *reinforcers*; responses that decrease the likelihood that the behavior will occur again are called *punishers*. The impact of any response is idiosyncratic, so the same consequence can increase the behavior in one person and diminish it in another. So, if your teen feels good when praised, praise might increase the likelihood that a behavior will happen again. If, however, she's uncomfortable being praised, her behaviors may decrease after she's praised. In order to assess whether your response is reinforcing or punishing, you'll have to develop an awareness of how behaviors change in reaction to your responses.

Reinforcers Are More Effective than Punishers

Punishment, taking something away that a teen wants to have (like computer time) or having her do something she doesn't want to do (like extra chores), is often not effective in diminishing behavior and may cause your teen to continue her behavior while making sure she doesn't "get caught." Punishment doesn't teach her what's expected and how you want her *to* behave. It's generally more effective to reinforce (with extra privileges, smiles, or an easy tone, for example) the teen for engaging in healthy and safe behaviors and when she's meeting expectations, than to punish her (with loss of privileges, harsh words, and so on) when she is not.

Parents often believe that it's necessary to punish unwanted behaviors; they think it's the most effective way to change behaviors, and they continue to use negative consequences even when they don't seem to be working. Decades of psychological research prove that punishment is *not* the most effective way to change behavior, and yet this is not widely known to, or accepted by, parents. Even when parents are aware that punishment doesn't work, they may still use it as a response to their own frustration. What *does* work is noticing and rewarding healthy and desirable behaviors; this is the most effective way to change behavior and results in increased cooperation and goodwill in families as well. At the same time, this can be challenging to implement.

If finding effective reinforcers for your teen is difficult—either because there isn't anything she wants or she already has everything she needs—look at the privileges you give her (such as electronics or activities) that she may take for granted, and have her earn them by meeting responsibilities and expectations. Although this may be a difficult lesson for a teen who is used to having whatever she wants, it's an important life lesson that privileges are *earned*, not simply given.

Parent attention may also be reinforcing to teens, even if the teen denies this is the case. Teens often appear uninterested in your reactions, and you may think that your attention doesn't matter. However, attention of any kind can be a valuable and potent reward and can result in an increase in behavior, even if this isn't your desired result. If, for example, you do not respond to requests from your teen to talk because you are too busy at that moment, then respond with a reprimand when your teen begins demanding and yelling, you might be inadvertently increasing the likelihood that your teen will demand and yell the next time she wants your attention. This means that it's important for you to be aware of what you respond to (even in a nonsupportive way) and to focus on giving attention to your teen most often when she's behaving in safe and effective ways. If you talk about or give attention to negative or unsafe behaviors (even to self-harm, unless it needs medical attention), you may be inadvertently reinforcing behaviors that would be more effective, in the long run, to ignore. You can be a very powerful reinforcer to your teen and, therefore, instrumental in shaping and changing behaviors by choosing what to respond to and what to ignore.

Natural Consequences

Natural consequences are those responses that occur in the real world, not those implemented by you. If your teen fails a test that she didn't study for or gets into trouble with the authorities for shoplifting, she is experiencing natural consequences to her behaviors. Ongoing exposure to natural consequences helps teens learn what happens when they make unsafe choices and/or have poor judgment. While your urge may be to protect your teen from these consequences, you may need to allow some of them to occur so that she learns from the experience (remember that you'll continue to intervene when safety is a concern). If you intervene by minimizing or otherwise eliminating these natural consequences, she learns that she can behave however she chooses, that she doesn't have to take responsibility for her actions, and that rules that apply to others don't apply to her. As hard or as scary as it might be for you to witness your teen experiencing natural consequences, the lesson learned is invaluable and may help shape her toward a healthier future.

Intermittent Reinforcement

Intermittent reinforcement is when rewards are given sometimes, but not always, following a behavior. An example is the way a slot machine's payout occurs occasionally and randomly, yet keeps the gambler engaged in pulling the lever. This type of reinforcement is powerful and contributes to very persistent behaviors. When, even against your better judgment, you give in to your teen's demands intermittently, she will continue to repeat the behavior in the hope that the next time will be the one that results in her getting what she wants. For example, if you say no to your teen over and over and then change your mind after she persists in her request—perhaps by becoming more abusive or threatening—she learns that if she is persistent enough or abusive enough, you'll eventually give her what she wants.

Intermittent reinforcement results in what you might experience as "unrelenting" behaviors because your teen is never sure when her behavior will result in her getting what she wants, much like a gambler never knows which pull on a slot machine will result in winning. If you feel unsure about the limit or unclear that you can maintain it, take time to think about how you want to respond until you can be certain and consistent so you don't ultimately reinforce persistence or threats by saying yes eventually when you initially may have said no. For example, if your teen asks permission to go somewhere and you don't want her to go, although it would not cause significant problems if she did, you might be tempted to say no initially and then give in after repeated demands. This inconsistent response ("no, no, no, yes") reinforces demanding and persistent behavior and keeps your teen thinking that you will give in eventually. Be clear about the limits you *can* observe (in which you will maintain your position regardless of what your teen continues to demand) and about your priorities (those issues that are so important, such as safety concerns, that if a battle with your teen results, you will still maintain your position) so that you don't give in when your teen "ups the ante" or wears you down, which would cause her to become even more persistent in the future. Consistent limits and follow-through are keys to effective parenting.

Change Comes Gradually

Consider what happens when your teen's room has become so dirty—with dirty dishes, food containers, and clothes strewn all over the floor—that it is unhealthy. If you tell your teen to "clean it up," she may be overwhelmed and not know where to start. Some behaviors may be complex or include multiple steps, and your teen may not be able to complete them, or she may become so frustrated trying to that she gives up. If you're reinforcing a new behavior, you want the teen to experience success and reward so that the behavior continues. So, at first, you may want to reinforce smaller increments of the behavior. For example, if your teen is frustrated by her inability to complete a big school project and has given up and refused to do any of it, you can calmly validate her frustration and then help her divide the work into more manageable parts, reinforcing and praising each small step she takes toward completion of the assignment. Likewise, help her take small steps toward cleaning up her room. She doesn't need to complete the whole project to experience success and reward. This translates into more willingness to attempt future projects.

Parent Behaviors Are Influenced by Their Teens

Parents are equally susceptible to behavioral principles, and your behaviors may increase or decrease based on the ways your teen responds to them. If your teen responds violently whenever she's told she can't do something, you may be so punished by this that you may hesitate to set limits even if you want to. If a usually irritable teen becomes friendlier when she gets what she wants, you may respond positively to requests you might otherwise have denied. When you can recognize that you might feel punished or reinforced by your teen and don't allow her responses to influence you, you'll be better able to parent in a consistent and effective manner.

It Can Get Worse Before It Gets Better

As you make changes in your parenting behaviors, your teen—in an effort to get you to respond in ways she's more comfortable and familiar with—may respond with an *increase* in the behaviors you're trying to decrease or in her angry behaviors toward you. Her behaviors will make it very hard for you to maintain your new behaviors. This increase in the frequency and intensity of her behavior is to be expected. When you maintain your behaviors, hers will diminish over time. Although it's understandable that you may want to give up, when you persist through this predictable "worsening" of her behavior and let your teen know that negative behaviors will not get her what she wants, you are laying the foundation for the possibility of significant change within the family.

Using Reinforcement and Punishment to Change Behaviors

Returning to the previous vignette, let's look at how Sheila's parents might respond to her behaviors. The first step is to identify the behavior(s) they want to change. Sheila's parents will prioritize these behaviors:

- attending therapy at least once a week

- taking prescribed medications

- diminishing her threatening behaviors

The second step is to identify what consequences usually follow the behavior. At the present time, there is no reinforcer in place for Sheila if she attends therapy or takes her meds, and no negative consequence if she does not. At times, Sheila's parents inadvertently reinforce her threatening behavior when they give in to her demands.

The third step is to consider what reinforcers or punishers can be used to increase or decrease the behaviors that are to be changed. Sheila's parents will do several things:

- stop giving Sheila money whenever she asks

- give her money for the activities she wants to attend only when she meets her responsibilities, attends therapy, or takes her meds

- no longer give in to her demands when she threatens

- ignore threats of self-harm

- have her assessed at a local emergency room or community mental health clinic if she continues to threaten suicide

- agree to match any money she makes at work or pay for her volunteer work by putting money in a spending account that she can have access to if she's also attending treatment

Strategically using reinforcement and punishment is sometimes difficult, especially when your teen is threatening or verbally or physically abusive. However, when you reinforce threatening or abusive behaviors by attending to or giving in to them, you'll ensure that they'll continue, which is the opposite of your goal. Effective parenting using strategies we have been discussing involves these components:

- identifying the specific behaviors you want to change

- finding a way to reinforce healthier behaviors

- not intermittently reinforcing threats or negative behaviors

- staying focused on the long-term benefits of remaining consistent and reinforcing safe and healthy behaviors

- being consistent over a long period of time

- understanding and accepting that there is some initial risk that the behaviors will increase or become more dangerous, and that the behaviors of the teen may get worse before they get better

---

Parent Practice: Changing Behaviors

If you want to change one or more behaviors, follow the prompts below and write your responses on a piece of paper or in a journal.

- What behavior do you want to change? Describe the behavior specifically.

- What consequences usually follow the behavior? How do you generally respond?

- Do you want to increase or decrease the behavior? Will you use reinforcement or punishment? Can you reinforce a positive behavior that can replace a less adaptive behavior?

- What specific consequence(s) will you use that you can apply consistently? List the reinforcers or punishers that you will use.

- After you have implemented the new consequence over time, write down the long-term consequences.

Strategy: Helping You and Your Teen Manage Stress

To be able to parent effectively, you must find the time and the ways to take care of yourself. If you wonder if you can spare the time to do things for yourself when your teen has so many pressing needs, think about the flight attendant who reminds passengers that they should put their own oxygen masks on before taking care of anyone else. You cannot parent effectively when you don't have the emotional or physical resources to do so.

Teens can be taught how to manage their emotional upheavals using skills that help them cope without making the situation worse (Linehan 1993a, 1993b; Miller, Rathus, and Linehan 2007). Parents can also learn to use these skills to calm down or distract themselves in difficult circumstances so that they can reduce the intensity of their own emotions and parent more effectively.

Distracting and Self-Soothing

Conventional wisdom holds that if you have something bothering you, talking about it helps. This is true sometimes; at other times, talking about something painful or difficult maintains or exacerbates the feelings and doesn't provide relief. What you might need instead is some time away from the situation to lessen the intensity of the emotion so that you can return to the situation later and be more effective at problem solving.

When you use coping skills (which we will discuss further in chapter 9) and take time to calm, distract, or soothe yourself, you'll be better able to respond to your teen effectively when you return to the situation. You'll also be modeling healthier ways to manage feelings for your teen.

Helping Your Teen Distract and Self-Soothe

Your teen or young adult might find that self-harm, using substances, yelling, or throwing things provides immediate relief. However, the problem is often made worse by these behaviors because the unintended consequences (hospitalization, loss of privileges and trust, trouble with the law, and so on) might be more detrimental, and the teen might experience shame or guilt afterward. Teens can learn to use skills to reduce their emotional intensity so that they can respond more effectively.

How can you coach your teen to use these strategies to help her calm down when she's reacting emotionally? When emotions are strong, teens don't always respond well to coaching suggestions from parents—suggestions that sometimes actually escalate situations. Instead of you, it may be the teen's therapist (if she has one) or someone she trusts who can coach her when she's highly emotional. What you *can* do is share strategies that you have found helpful and see if your teen will practice them with you. Accept her answer if she says no. Practice together if she says yes. Another strategy might be to have a discussion with her when she's calm and ask if there are ways that you can help her when she's upset. And do try to validate her feelings (see chapter 2, "Validation"), even if it seems as though she isn't listening.

Don't be surprised if your teen tells you that she wants to be left alone when she's upset. Often teens will leave the presence of family in order to calm down. Leaving the situation might actually be a strategy! Let your teen choose what works for her, and let her use strategies in ways that are most effective. Let her know that you'll be available when and if she wants to talk to you. Be available, willing to listen, and validating when she's ready and willing to talk, and provide suggestions only if she asks or accepts them willingly.

Skills to Distract or Self-Soothe During Stressful Times

Pick a skill or skills that might work for you. Different skills may work at different times, depending on the level of stress or immediate need.

- *Play sports or exercise.*

- *Speak to a friend.*

- *Listen to music.*

- *Write in a journal.*

- *Read a book.*

- *Work on a puzzle or play a nonviolent computer game.*

- *Imagine you're at a special and calming place; remember a vacation spot or situation you enjoyed.*

- *Drink warm tea.*

- *Take a warm bath or shower.*

- *Watch a funny TV show or movie (not a depressing or sad one).*

- *Use nice-smelling lotion.*

- *Pet an animal.*

- *Listen to nature sounds.*

- *Eat a special food that you enjoy (and that does not make you feel guilty).*

Strategy: Communicating Effectively

Parents sometimes wonder how they can communicate and interact with their teen in ways that increase the likelihood that she'll hear and acknowledge what's being said or asked. Often teens and their parents, each focused on different goals and responding to different needs and priorities, have a difficult time staying wise and not getting distracted by emotions and differences. This section will focus on how you might use strategies to get your needs met, to increase the likelihood that you can effectively ask for something or say no to a request while still maintaining the relationship and your own self-respect (Linehan 1993b). These skills will be very helpful in effectively communicating with your teen.

Establishing the Priorities of Your Interaction

People may not always realize what they are trying to accomplish when they begin an interaction with others. When you're communicating with your teen or young adult, your goal(s) may be to (1) request something or express your own needs, (2) deny a request, (3) maintain or repair the relationship itself, (4) simply be with your teen in ways that you enjoy, and/or (5) behave or respond in ways that respect your values and enhance your own self-respect (Linehan 1993b). If you aren't clear about what you're trying to accomplish, you may walk away disappointed without really knowing why. When you are clear about your goals, you can prioritize which are most important—those goals will get your attention and focus first. When you have several goals, knowing which goal you want to address first (that is, which goal is your priority) before you begin an interaction helps you stay focused and not be distracted by other needs. You'll be more effective in getting your goals met in this manner.

In order to establish your priorities, you will first have to be mindful by slowing down and noticing what's happening. Then assess the situation and determine what in the long run you want to accomplish. Using this awareness, you can establish your priorities. For example, if your teen is unsafe, you may not prioritize getting homework done, whereas if your teen is safe, homework may become a priority.

In the vignette at the beginning of this chapter, Sheila's parents wanted to let her know that she would not be getting a privilege (concert tickets) when she did not meet their expectations. This was contrary to what Sheila wanted and expected from them. In this situation, Sheila's parents have a specific goal—getting Sheila to meet their expectations—that is their priority. Maintaining the relationship might be a secondary and slightly less important priority, and her parents might have to accept that Sheila may be unhappy with their response and angry at them.

Parent Practice: Planning an Interaction

Ask yourself the following questions. Write your answers on a separate piece of paper or in your journal.

- What do I want to accomplish?

    - Do I want to ask for something I want or need?

    - Do I want to tell my teen what I expect of her?

    - Do I want to deny a request?

    - Do I simply want to enjoy time with my kid?

- If there's a lot going on, what is my *highest priority*?

Putting It All Together

Though you may find it hard to believe, you can ask for what you want, keep a strong relationship with your teen, and feel okay with yourself afterward. Here's the most effective way to ask for what you want or to express your needs or expectations (Linehan, 1993b):

- Describe the situation to provide a context and to explain why you want what you're asking for. ("Your grades have been slipping, and I am concerned that you aren't studying enough.")

- Make your request or say no clearly. ("I really want you to do some studying tonight" or "I'm not giving you permission to go to the party because you need to study.")

- Stay focused on your top priority and don't bring up other issues that may cloud it or distract you from it.

- Acknowledge your appreciation of your teen or provide an incentive or concrete reinforcer if she meets your request.

- Remain confident in your request and assert yourself.

- Decide if you're willing to negotiate and know, in advance, what your limits are.

At the same time, in order to maintain the relationship, you'll want to do these things:

- Listen, with genuine interest, to what your teen says to you.

- Validate her feelings.

- Try to be as relaxed as possible.

And in order to maintain positive feelings about yourself and how you handle the situation, here are some guidelines to think about:

- Maintain your own values and morals throughout the interaction. Do not say or do things that will make you feel ashamed when the interaction is over.

- Do not apologize for what you're saying or doing.

- Remain truthful and honest. Even though you might want to lie rather than honestly express how you feel or what you want, this would do little to build trust and might leave you feeling disappointed in yourself.

Keeping these guidelines for communicating effectively in mind, the vignette of Sheila and her parents can provide insights and ideas that you might find helpful. When asked to buy the concert tickets, Sheila's parents could answer, calmly and gently, by explaining their response to her and validating her as a way to maintain the relationship: "We know how much you want to go to the concert and we know you'll be disappointed if you don't go. At this time, you haven't earned the money because you haven't met the expectations we asked of you. We'll be happy to give you money and other privileges when you meet some of your responsibilities. Is there some way that we can help you meet some expectations so that you can do the things you want to do?" Sheila's parents will be most effective if they stay firm on not giving her money, do not make apologies for their decision, and are not distracted by her emotions or threats.

When Strategies Don't Work

Using these strategies may *increase* the possibility that you'll get what you want, although it doesn't guarantee that you will. The other person may deny your request, even when it's made skillfully, or decide that other considerations come first. Your teen can deny your requests, refuse to meet your expectations, and continue to treat you disrespectfully regardless of how much *you* use these strategies. Or she may not want to spend time with you even when you may be validating and supportive. You or your teen may be disappointed when using strategies doesn't get needs met. Other skills may be necessary to manage this disappointment.

Remember that your teen's immediate response may not be her ultimate response. You may find that she leaves an interaction angry or dismissive, only to return the next day with a new and more cooperative attitude. To be effective doesn't always mean that you get what you want in the moment; it means that you plant seeds and express yourself in ways that *increase the likelihood* that your teen will hear you and think about what you said or what you asked. You may not succeed in every interaction, and yet expressing your needs to your teen, establishing expectations and limits, and finding ways to maintain your relationship are all important in parenting her over the long haul into adulthood.

How Do You Want to Feel?

You cannot always control how your teen will react, no matter how skillfully you try to interact. You can only control your own behaviors so that you can still feel okay about *yourself* when the interaction is over. You will feel better if you remain focused on being nonjudgmental and acting wisely, and if you don't get caught up in your teen's emotionality.

You may become aware that an interaction is no longer skillful and has little potential to be effective. If your teen needs to walk away, let her go. If you need to walk away, you may find that taking time-outs is very effective for parents, too! Don't demand that communication continue when it's no longer effective. While you may feel like your teen is "winning" and you're "giving in," you'll actually feel better if you can walk away, at least for the moment. There will be other opportunities to return to the discussion when emotions are less intense, and the interaction may be more effective then.

Parent Practice: Using Strategies to Interact Effectively

Write your responses to these questions on a piece of paper or in a journal.

Imagine a situation in which you want to ask your teen for something.

- Describe what you want, why you want it, and why it's important.

- What are you willing to negotiate? What are your limits?

- How will you express and show your appreciation to your teen if she meets your request?

Imagine a situation in which you want to express your values to your teen.

- What value do you want to emphasize in your interaction?

- What will you say that is truthful and doesn't apologize for your position?

Summary

In this chapter, we described strategies that will help you understand and then change your responses to your teen in order to parent more effectively.

Key Points:

- Weigh the positive and negative consequences of decisions, taking into consideration both immediate and long-term goals.

- Use the story of emotion to lessen emotionality and respond more effectively.

- Use the principles of reinforcement and punishment strategically to increase healthy behaviors and to decrease unsafe behaviors.

- Consider what you most want to accomplish when interacting with your teen and stay focused on those priorities.

Chapter 4

Balanced Parenting

As a parent of a young person in general and a young person who has intense emotions in particular, you, like other parents, may often be pulled into power struggles that involve all-or-nothing thinking. Both you and your teen may engage in rigid thinking in which you may see things in terms of either/or, good/bad, right/wrong, or fair/unfair. When your teen has intense emotions, he may idealize some people and demonize others, feel totally competent one minute and worthless the next, want total independence at some times and be totally dependent at others, push you away one moment and then be relentlessly demanding of your attention the next. You, too, may get caught up in this "it has to be my way" thinking. You may become emotionally reactive to your teen's way of thinking and may vacillate between extreme responses.

In this chapter, we'll look at ways to lessen these power struggles and to help you and other family members find a way to move forward when you feel stuck. We'll discuss a balanced approach to parenting, which helps you to accept the validity in contradictory positions and perspectives. This approach enables you to find a synthesis or a "middle path" and parent more effectively (Miller, Rathus, and Linehan 2007).

Finding a Middle Path: Dialectical Thinking

Dialectical thinking means acknowledging that there is validity in different perspectives; it provides a way to synthesize the inevitable contradictions that exist in the real world, and between people, so that a new path—a middle path—can be forged. It also means decreasing extreme, absolute, and/or rigid thinking so that you can accept, and entertain, multiple perspectives. You and your teen see things differently and often have contradictory goals, which frequently leads to power struggles as you each try to convince the other that you're "right." You may often feel stuck and unable to move forward. Finding a middle path through dialectical thinking helps minimize these power struggles as you and your teen let go of your rigid positions and seek a solution or understanding that works for both of you. The ideas below will help you find that middle path by using dialectical thinking:

- There is more than one valid point of view in experiencing situations, circumstances, people, and even history.

- It's useful to avoid seeing things as "all good" or "all bad."

- Change is possible and probable.

- Meaning and truth change over time.

- The way things are today can change tomorrow.

Family Dynamics and Multiple Perspectives

You, like other parents, may often be confused by what you witness in your teen. Because a teen's brain and body are developing, he's in a state of constant change. When you accept this notion of constant change, it's easier for you to develop ways to respond that (1) are consistent and flexible, (2) promote independence even as you remain available when necessary, and (3) provide structure and limits while accepting that your teen will experiment and make various different choices.

You may often find yourself fighting with your coparent or your children, trying to prove that what you believe or want to do is right and that you know best. You expend energy debating that your truth is the *real* truth. At the same time, other family members try to convince *you* that their truth is the real truth. This struggle tends to lead only to more struggle. When the world is perceived in an extreme right/wrong or either/or manner, the only alternative to being right is being wrong. People fight dearly to *not* be wrong and to make sure that others agree with them or validate their position. This is even clearer in families; teens often want their parents to agree with them because disagreement means they're wrong, which feels intolerable. Conflict often occurs between parents as each tries to convince the other that his or her ideas on parenting are best. What helps minimize these struggles is accepting that there may be multiple perspectives and seeking what's valid in each point of view—in short, *accepting that one does not always have to be right in order not to be wrong.*

Choosing the Middle Path: How to Think Dialectically

Very specific and practical tools can help you change the way you speak and communicate and, therefore, help you think more dialectically. By using these tools, you will be better able to find a middle path that will lead you to more balanced parenting. One of the easiest ways to move from rigid thinking to dialectical thinking is to practice *not* using the word "but." Instead, use the word "and" whenever and wherever possible. Think about the different meanings in these statements:

I'm happy you did well on your exam, but you still have to keep studying.

I'm happy that you did well on your exam, *and* I still want you to keep studying.

Or these:

I'm proud of you much of the time, but I'm disappointed in how you just behaved.

I'm proud of you much of the time, *and* I'm disappointed in how you just behaved.

In the sentences using "but," the first part of the sentence is dismissed by the second part. Your teen walks away remembering only what he needs to do or that you're disappointed in him. Using "and" gives validity to all perspectives. Practice dialectical thinking by making this small, and yet significant, change in the way you speak. When parents begin to incorporate this powerful change—using "and" instead of "but"—they remark that their view of the world, their ability to accept contradictions, and the way they think and communicate with their teen is very different. Consider these additional ways to think more dialectically (Miller, Rathus, and Linehan 2007):

- Use "both/and" thinking instead of either/or thinking. For example, consider that your child can be *both* kind *and* self-centered rather than *either* kind *or* self-centered.

- Minimize use of absolute terms such as "always," "never," "everyone," "nobody," or variations of these words.

- Be willing to look at alternatives and accept other opinions as valid, even if they're different from yours or you don't agree with them.

- Avoid statements such as "That's just the way it is" and substitute "I think [or I feel] _____."

In the chart that follows we present some examples of dialectical and nondialectical statements. Notice how (1) the nondialectical statements reflect the black-and-white thinking often seen in teens with intense emotions, and (2) the dialectical statements do not contain absolute words and accept alternative or more balanced perspectives.

Nondialectical Statements	Dialectical Statements
I trust everyone. *Or* I don't trust anyone.	I trust some people and find it hard to trust other people.
I can't do anything well. *Or* Things always come easily to me.	Some things are easy for me and some things are a challenge.
I can't stand it if you hurt me. *Or* It's no big deal if you hurt me.	I get angry when you hurt me and I still love you.

The Challenges of Polarized Thinking for Parents and Teens

Like most parents and teens, you and your teen will sometimes become polarized in your thinking and in the ways that you respond to each other, creating dialectical dilemmas—choices between equally untenable and extreme positions. When your teen has intense emotions, the patterns can become more rigid and the struggles more powerful, as you each dig in on your perspective. Rigid or extreme responses are rarely effective in the long run and can be disruptive to family interactions. You may even take one extreme position when your coparent takes the other, as you strive to compensate for each other. This usually creates more conflict and confusion. As circumstances and emotions change, or as you or your teen feel you're not achieving what you want, you may find that you move from one extreme to the other. You and your teen may vacillate between extreme positions on these issues (Miller, Rathus, and Linehan 2007):

- responding to typical adolescent behaviors as if they're problems, or responding to problematic behaviors as if they're typical

- being overly lenient, having too few expectations and limits, or exercising too much control or being too strict

- giving too much autonomy and freedom or holding on and not allowing enough independence while, possibly, fostering dependency

If you find yourself reacting in extreme or rigid ways, or vacillating between extremes, you'll parent more effectively when you (1) are more balanced, less extreme, and find ways to compromise; (2) respond to behaviors wisely rather than emotionally; (3) find a way to assess behaviors in the moment without fears about the past or future; and (4) learn what's typical of adolescence (and what's not), keeping in mind that adolescence is a time of experimentation, rebellion, and focus on the peer group.

Difficult Choices: Responding to Your Teen's Behaviors

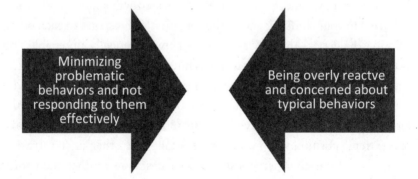

Minimizing problematic behaviors and not responding to them effectively

Being overly reactve and concerned about typical behaviors

You may find yourself overreacting to behaviors that are fairly common among young people (for example, eye rolling, talking back, disrespectful language, and so on), and at the same or other times, you may notice that you dismiss or ignore behaviors that are quite problematic (drug abuse, sexual risk taking, self-harming, and so on). How you view behaviors and respond to them is often influenced by your own upbringing, the past behaviors of your teen, and/or by your family's mental health history. If your teen has a history of aggression, you might be more concerned about his slamming a door than another parent. If there's a history of mental illness in your family, you may either overreact to or dismiss behaviors as a way to manage your own fears. You might also dismiss problematic behaviors or become overly vigilant about typical behaviors if a sibling has emotional difficulties or dangerous behaviors. When you react to or dismiss behaviors based on your history or emotions, your parenting will be less effective and more friction will develop in your family.

When your teen has intense emotions, you develop a high threshold for behavior problems, because they may have been going on for so long. Or you may focus your attention on school issues, which seem more manageable, when drug use or self-harm may be more problematic. You may excuse problematic behaviors as your teen "simply being a teen" as a way to normalize or dismiss them because you feel so powerless to change them. On the other end of the spectrum, you may be so overwhelmed by the dangerousness of your teen's behavior that you find it easier to focus on or worry about more mundane or typical daily living problems. It's easy to see how your perspective on what's typical or what's problematic can become skewed when there is intense emotionality. And in order to parent effectively, it's important to have clarity about the behaviors that will be your priorities, such as safety, and make your decisions wisely rather than emotionally.

Extreme responses create their own problems for you. If you dismiss problematic behaviors, you won't get your teen the help that might be needed and you may inadvertently allow your teen to continue to engage in dangerous activity. On the other hand, if you're overly worried about typical behaviors, you might stifle your teen's development, create more anxiety for yourself, and/or create friction when acceptance might be more effective.

Balanced Responses

To decide if a behavior is a problem, consider the behavior itself, the intensity of how it's presented, the risk of the behavior, and the ways in which the behavior dominates or interferes with the overall life of your teen. In addition, consider why a behavior occurs; ask whether a particular behavior may be part of a teen's normal experimentation, like drinking alcohol at a party, or whether the behavior is a way to manage painful emotions, like drinking alone and secretly. While both behaviors are cause for concern, the way you respond will be different. Seek professional mental health care for your teen if you're worried about the dangerous nature of your teen's behavior.

The chart that follows shows examples of typical and problem behaviors.

Typical Behaviors	Problem Behaviors
Returning from school and staying in his room until dinner	Sleeping whenever not in school
Experimenting sexually with peers from school	Meeting sexual partners from the Internet in secret
Fighting with his parents	Breaking things or acting aggressively when limits are set
Experiencing anxiety about decisions	Being paralyzed by indecision
Experiencing stress at school, feeling overwhelmed	Refusing to go to school

In order to lessen the power struggles, tension, and difficulties that result from overconcern about typical behaviors—or from the opposite, dismissing or ignoring problematic behaviors—look at the ways that you can move more toward the middle and a more balanced approach.

If you tend to overreact to typical adolescent behaviors, you'll need to increase your recognition of what's typical for teens and decrease seeing typical behaviors as problematic. You can do this in several ways:

- Talk to other parents, attend parent workshops, or use the information in the chart to find out what's typical and what's not.

- Consider the function of the behavior and respond with less worry if the behavior is not dangerous or disruptive.

- Think wisely about whether the behavior occurs in social situations and is related to teen experimentation or identity development.

If your teen goes to a party and returns having used alcohol or drugs, you might become worried that he is behaving in a way that will create more issues in the future and you might want to react with anger. However, when you step back, slow down, and consider that teens tend to experiment at parties, you may respond in a less reactive and more effective manner as you talk to your teen about substance use.

If you tend to minimize, dismiss, or treat as typical behaviors that others might see as problematic, you'll need to increase your identification of problematic behaviors and decrease your acceptance and dismissal of problematic behaviors. You can do this in several ways:

- Evaluate the risk and dangerousness of behaviors by thinking wisely and seeking help if you have concerns about the behavior.

- Ask yourself if the behavior can lead to significant unsafe, maladaptive, or legal consequences.

- Think wisely about whether or not these behaviors are being used to help your teen regulate his intense emotions.

You'll develop more balanced and less extreme responses when you understand and accept what behavior is typical—even if you find it challenging and frustrating—and what behavior is outside of the norm and then respond accordingly. Finding a balance may be challenging and will depend on the unique variables of each situation, and at the same time, it will provide you with useful structure and guidance to respond effectively.

What's It Like for Your Teen?

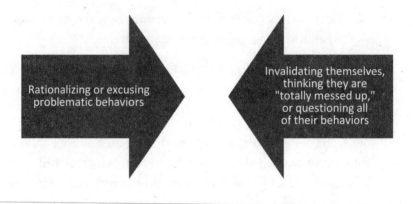

Teens, too, struggle around the issue of whether or not their behaviors are normal. You may be very confused by the inconsistency you see in your teen's behavior. It helps when you understand the ways in which he may vacillate between accepting his behaviors as "fine" or seeing himself as "messed up."

In order to feel normal and not feel different, some young people may, at times, excuse, rationalize, or dismiss problematic behaviors by saying they're similar to those of their friends. ("So what if I blacked out after the party—it happens to all my friends.") It's hard for any teen to accept that he may have a problem and be different than his peers, so he may deny he has any problems. Other teens may take the other extreme response and see themselves as "total screw-ups" who don't behave like a typical teen ever and who will have problems forever, feeling hopeless as a result. ("I just can't do anything right. Everyone else knows how to do this work and it's just impossible for me. I'll never be able to do it.") They invalidate their feelings and experiences in the ways that they may have felt invalidated by others. You may be even more confused when your teen vacillates between these extreme responses just as you do between your own.

It helps to understand the dynamics that drive these different extreme responses in your teen. This enables you to provide the wise responses that will help your teen find some balance for himself.

Extreme Responses: Leniency and Strictness

Making too few demands or having too few expectations or limits, being overly lenient

Exercising too much control, being too strict, having too many lmits or being overly punitive

You may have a parenting style that tends to be more lenient, minimizing rules, expectations, and demands and allowing your teen to have more freedoms and to make more of his own decisions. Or you may have a parenting style that is stricter, less trusting, more demanding, and more punitive. You may want to have more control over your teen's behavior. If your teen has intense emotions and the resulting behavior problems, you may react in ways that are exaggerations of your natural parenting style, or you may develop an entirely different way of parenting.

If, for example, your teen or young adult becomes intensely emotional, self-harming, threatening, or abusive whenever there's a limit, denial, or request, you may become so fatigued and so afraid of the possibility of an aggressive or violent outburst that you avoid setting limits altogether. While you may recognize that this isn't effective—because it gives your teen free rein without the limits that are necessary to guide him while also giving him the message that causing fear in others will get him what he wants—it's understandable that you might avoid these reactions by acting more leniently than you otherwise might have.

On the other hand, you may become more controlling of your teen, making stricter demands and increasing limits when you're afraid that your teen's impulsive, risk-taking, or dangerous behaviors will lead to very serious consequences. Under these circumstances, it's also easy to see how you might want to exercise more control over his behavioral decisions to keep him safe, surprising even yourself when you deny requests that other parents would allow without any hesitation. You might wrestle with how to keep your teen safe while trying to maintain some peace within your home.

You may also vacillate between these two extreme behaviors. Parental fatigue, ongoing battles with your teen, and uncontrolled emotional outbursts may lead you to give up and let your teen do whatever he wants. When you see your teen's behaviors become more unsafe without limits or controls, you may go to the other extreme and respond in a more controlling manner. Moving from extreme response to extreme response is not effective and actually leads to more unsafe behaviors in your teen.

Balanced Responses

Your goal is to balance providing structure and guidance with a willingness to take some risks by allowing your teen to make some of his own decisions. Your teen will need both limits and freedoms in order to move through the developmental tasks of adolescence.

If you think that you're reacting too leniently and that you allow your teen to do whatever he wants, even if it goes against your values (for example, by not reacting when your teen uses drugs in your home) or puts other members of your family at risk (for example, allowing your teen to bring strangers into your home), you may have to move toward a more authoritative way of responding. You can do this by taking these actions:

- Calmly and clearly discuss your rules, limits, expectations, and potential consequences.

- Do not give permission for activities that you don't agree with or that you think may be dangerous for your teen or others in your family.

- Follow through on what you say and what you expect without giving in if your teen's behaviors become more challenging or aggressive.

- Treat your teen with respect and love while establishing your expectations.

You may need to withstand some unpleasant behaviors as your teen tries to get you to give him what he wants. It will be hard, at first, to make these changes, especially when your teen responds with emotional intensity. And to put it dialectically: in order to parent effectively, making these changes, while hard, is necessary.

If you have become more controlling in reaction to your teen's potentially unsafe choices and decisions, you'll need to decrease your control and increase your teen's self-determination and ability to make his own decisions by taking some risks. You can do this by taking these actions:

- Set and observe limits wisely so that you're focused on those that are most important.

- Discuss with your teen how he can make safe and skillful choices as you allow him to take more control.

- Let your teen know he'll be allowed more freedoms and privileges as he shows responsibility in making safe choices and be prepared to give him those privileges.

- Take the risk of letting him make some choices on his own and continue to allow more freedoms as he earns your trust.

Examples of Balanced Responses

Situation A: Your teen is found at a party that he didn't have permission to attend and at which there was drinking and drug use. You may now feel that you can no longer trust him and, as a result, you limit his unsupervised activities with friends. As time passes, your teen begins to request more freedom. You may gradually relinquish control and increase his privileges by taking the following incremental steps, increasing his privileges as he responds to the increased level of trust:

1. Drop him off and pick him up at a specific time and in a public place after a limited time.

2. Increase time he's allowed to be with friends.

3. Allow attendance at a chaperoned party, after confirming with parents.

4. Allow more independence in activity choices.

5. Allow more freedom in his coming and going from chosen activities.

Situation B: You discover that your teen is posting sexualized pictures of herself on a website. You may respond by taking away Internet access. After some time, she requests access to the Internet again. You don't yet trust her and want to institute some guidelines:

1. Provide limited, supervised access to the Internet after she's agreed to let you check history and postings.

2. Increase time allowed on the Internet.

3. Allow Internet use in private and without supervision while still checking history and postings.

4. Allow more unsupervised Internet use on a limited basis while trusting her to access only approved sites.

5. Increase the amount of unsupervised and unchecked Internet use.

In these two examples, the teen can gradually and successfully earn back privileges, freedom, and parental trust.

Letting go of some of your control and allowing your teen more freedom will create more anxiety for you, especially in the beginning. Likewise, there will be anxiety and fears if you begin to set limits that your teen reacts angrily to. In chapter 9, we'll provide some ways for you to manage your anxiety in these situations so that they don't interfere with balanced and effective parenting.

Balanced responses will ultimately reflect that there are times you'll want to be more lenient, and other times where you'll need to exercise more parental control. You'll do what works in a given situation, weighing all the variables and acting wisely. You will *both* set limits *and* allow your teen to make independent decisions, strategically moving from one to the other as necessary.

What's It Like for Your Teen?

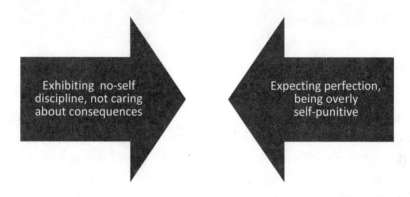

Exhibiting no-self discipline, not caring about consequences

Expecting perfection, being overly self-punitive

Your teen is developing the ability to respond effectively to challenges, and may find himself struggling to respond to expectations (both yours and his) in a consistent and balanced way. He may, at times, be too tough on himself or have unrealistic, perfectionistic expectations for himself. At other times, he may not take things seriously enough and will be too undisciplined to complete his responsibilities. Either extreme is ineffective and leaves him unhappy and disappointed with the outcome.

You might be startled by the apparent lack of concern about performance one moment and then the distress associated with performance the next. This is unsettling for both you and your teen, and the vacillation from one extreme to the other contributes to tension and conflict at home. Your validation of your teen's concerns and your desire that he meets expectations will help him develop a more balanced approach.

Extreme Responses: Encouraging Dependency or Encouraging Too Much Independence

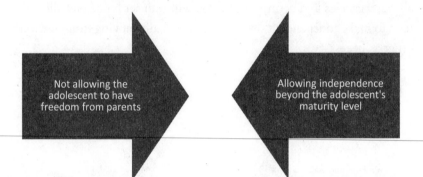

Not allowing the adolescent to have freedom from parents

Allowing independence beyond the adolescent's maturity level

Adolescents need to take risks, learn how to make their own decisions, and have opportunities in which they can develop their sense of who they are as they move toward adulthood. Learning how to function independently is a developmental task of adolescence and requires practice, experimentation, and opportunities to learn. Many parents find that letting teens test out new behaviors is anxiety provoking; when your teen has intense emotions and behaviors that may result (or might have already resulted) in problems, the fear and anxiety can become almost paralyzing. While you may recognize that you're stifling your teen's development or his natural desire to become more independent by not allowing him any freedoms, you may also be too afraid of the possible consequences to allow the natural and developmentally appropriate behaviors of adolescence to occur.

Or you may be overwhelmed by trying to parent a teen who demands freedom and independence by rejecting your input, structure, or guidance. As a result, you may allow your teen near-total independence without providing necessary support and guidance. You may withdraw from your parenting role before your teen is truly able to function independently. At times, this feels easier and may result in a more peaceful home, at least temporarily. It also means that your teen doesn't experience supportive opportunities to develop and assess independent behaviors. Nor does he learn how to ask for help when it might be needed or helpful. If you allow this freedom, you may become afraid over time that his poor judgment and decision making will create dangerous situations for him; you may then shift to the other extreme of holding on to your teen too tightly. It's understandable that these extreme behaviors develop, and it's also clear that these responses don't allow for a safe and healthy maturation process in your teen.

Neither extreme—of giving too much independence or no independence—will work over the long run. Yet you may find yourself picking one or the other or ineffectively and emotionally vacillating between the two approaches. The problem is how to allow age-appropriate freedoms while providing guidance and help and teaching your teen how to make safe, independent choices.

Balanced Responses

Your goal is to blend guidance and support in decision making with helping your teen become independent. To parent in a balanced and effective way, provide the safety net of being available for your teen when he needs help, provide guidance when he's learning new behaviors, and also allow him to have the opportunity to learn from his mistakes.

While it's more difficult to allow your teen independence when his decisions are not always safe, it's important for you to allow him to make some of his own choices so that he can learn how to manage independence and freedom. If you tend to foster dependency by making decisions for your teen and giving him minimal freedom, you may find a more balanced approach by taking these actions:

- Think wisely about what's typical behavior and give your teen the freedom to experiment with new behaviors in a gradual and skillful way.

- Teach your teen how to problem-solve through examples from your own life.

- Provide guidelines for your teen to make his own decisions by talking with him, weighing the pros and cons of his decisions, and acknowledging the possible consequences of different decisions.

- Be available to your teen to provide guidance when necessary, even if he may not recognize the need for it.

- Intervene, in consultation with your teen, if he needs help navigating situations that may come up at school, at a job, with friends, or elsewhere.

Be clear about what will both keep your teen safe in the short run and enable him to learn, grow, and develop in a healthy way in the long run. This is a very difficult task; it requires that you allow your teen to take small steps in the beginning and have more freedoms and choices as he shows that he can handle them responsibly.

If you have allowed your teen unlimited freedoms and independence that he may not be mature enough to handle skillfully and safely, you may find a balance by taking these actions:

- Negotiate with your teen about which freedoms he can have and which will be limited, using your own wise judgment in guiding this discussion.

- Be consistent in limiting some freedoms while not giving in when your teen's behaviors become aggressive or threatening.

- Discuss with your teen the importance of being able to ask for help, and model this behavior when possible.

- Be available to help when necessary and provide needed guidance.

Examples of Balanced Responses

Consider a situation in which your teen, who is a high school sophomore, wants to go to a party which will include some older kids. You don't want him to go because you're concerned that he won't be able to manage the peer pressure or the risks he may face. You want to say no. Then you also think about how you can help your adolescent learn how to manage these situations.

You talk to him about the possible situations he might face, problem-solve with him about how to manage these situations, and implement these rules and guidelines:

1. He will keep his phone with him—and turned on—at all times.

2. While at the party, he will periodically text you that he is okay.

3. If he has any problems during the party, he can call you at any time and you will pick him up—no questions asked.

4. He won't leave the party without talking to you first.

5. He'll be available to be picked up at the time that you agreed to.

In this way, you can allow him to have some freedom, teach him how to problem-solve, and also have some checks on his behaviors. If he is able to follow these guidelines, you can lessen some of the expectations the next time he asks to go to a party.

You'll find a balanced approach when you respond to your teen's behaviors with the understanding that he needs freedom and independence to grow and learn, *and at the same time*, he needs limits and structure to guide him through this newfound freedom. Striking the balance is the goal of effective parenting.

What's It Like for Your Teen?

Needing constant help or attention from parents or others, feeling helpless

Wanting to, and beleiving they can, take care of everything themselves, pushing others away

A developmental task of adolescence is to separate from you through a process of rebellion, experimentation, and independent decision making. However, just as the young child may take steps away from you while looking over his shoulder to make sure you're still there, your teen is reassured when you're still available at times when he needs help, guidance, or support. Your teen who has intense emotions will have an even more extreme response to his internal desire to be independent while still wanting to make sure that you are available when and if he needs you. Your teen may aggressively push you away or demand greater independence than he may be prepared for. Or he may feel overwhelmed by life and decision making and demand constant attention from you, seeming unable to make even simple decisions. It's easy to see how either extreme is a problem for you and your teen. If he becomes scared by too much independence or bristles with too much dependency, he may vacillate and move to the other extreme response.

You may be confused about how to respond when your teen pushes you away at times and then at other times demands immediate and constant attention and seems incapable of doing anything for himself. This is a natural process that becomes more exaggerated by emotional intensity. Your teen has a natural need to both experiment with independence and know that you'll still be available to help when needed. While it's hard to be pushed aside, don't take this behavior personally; it's a sign your teen is learning to be independent. At the same time, be available, even if it may be inconvenient, when your teen needs you. Your teen will benefit when you help him find a balance between practicing adult behaviors and getting the support and help that he, like everyone, still needs. This balance can help your teen become a healthy and self-reliant young adult.

Finding Overall Balanced Parenting

Having extreme responses or vacillating between extreme responses is not conducive to having a peaceful home or helping your teen develop into a healthy adult. While it may not always be apparent how to find a middle path, you will benefit from stepping back from situations and thinking about how to respond in a wise and balanced manner. You will find balance by taking these actions:

- Give your teen independence *and* provide support and guidance when it's needed or wanted.

- Give your teen choices, privileges, *and* limits.

- Let your teen "win some issues" by giving in *and* choose the priorities that are nonnegotiable.

- Treat your teen with firmness *and* gentleness.

- Provide your teen with the roots of belonging and the knowledge that you will be available when necessary *and* the wings to explore and learn about life on his own.

- Accept your teen for who he is *and* provide life lessons and expectations to guide him into a healthy adulthood.

Perhaps most importantly, you'll benefit from balancing acceptance of your teen as he is in this moment with the hope that change is possible and will make his life better. You will feel better if you accept that, while his future may not be the one you had hoped he would have, he can still have the life he wants to have.

Parent Practice: Moving Toward Balanced Parenting

Think about the issues discussed in this chapter and ask yourself what changes you need to make—what behaviors you can increase and which you will decrease—to find a more balanced approach. Write down your responses on a separate piece of paper or in a journal.

Summary

In this chapter, we discussed how to develop a more balanced approach to your parenting despite the inherent difficulties in parenting a teen who has intense emotions. We discussed the fears and concerns that often cause you to become rigid in your parenting responses or to vacillate between extreme positions. We then discussed conflicts that you may face and ways you can resolve these conflicts that will encourage your teen to safely navigate the normative tasks of adolescence despite his emotional intensity.

Key Points:

- Thinking and acting in a balanced, less extreme way helps you manage seemingly contradictory urges and perspectives. It helps you parent in a more balanced way by accepting that there is validity to the perspectives of other family members, even if you disagree with them.

- You may sometimes react in extreme ways when you're scared, worried, or fatigued, and these extreme responses are not usually effective.

- You can balance a tendency toward extreme positions by understanding the developmental tasks of adolescence, setting limits, providing structure while also being flexible, and by providing opportunities for your teen to have freedom as well as support and guidance.

Part 2

Responding to
Problem Behaviors

Chapter 5

Suicidal and Self-Harming Behaviors

This chapter will be relevant to you if your teen or young adult has exhibited any of the following behaviors: threats of suicide, suicide attempts, self-harming (cutting, burning, overdosing, head banging, and so on).

One of the most difficult, distressing, and painful experiences you can face as a parent is having a teen who expresses a desire not to live, makes suicidal attempts, or engages in any type of self-harm. If you are in this situation, you are, quite understandably, confused and scared by these behaviors, bewildered about how your teen could feel or behave this way, questioning if these behaviors may be "attention seeking," and afraid that your teen might actually kill herself. If your teen talks about wanting to die or self-harm, you may change how you parent, often making decisions and choices based on the fear that if you do the "wrong" thing, you'll cause your teen to hurt herself.

In this chapter, we will discuss ways in which you can effectively parent a teen or young adult whose desire to hurt herself may be as inexplicable to you as it is scary. We'll provide ways for you to navigate the need to respond to suicidal or self-harming behaviors in ways that don't reinforce the behavior *and* help keep your teen safe.

Understanding Suicidal and Self-Harming Behavior

There is a clinical distinction between suicidal behavior with the intent to die and nonsuicidal self-injury such as burning, cutting, overdosing, and other behaviors in which there is harm to the body although no intent to die. However, *all* self-harm, whether or not there is intent to die, is serious and dangerous, and it is the highest priority for clinical intervention and response from parents. Teens who self-harm are at an increased risk for suicide (Hawton and Harriss 2007). Teens who don't intend to kill themselves may unintentionally do so or accidentally or impulsively cause more damage than they intended.

It's important to make the distinction between the *intent* of a behavior and its *consequence*. Teens generally begin to self-harm or express suicidal urges to lessen emotional pain, among other reasons—not to get attention. However, even though the original intent of the behavior may have been to cope with painful emotions, the teen will inevitably receive attention for the behavior as parents increase their vigilance and try to keep her safe. Over time, the teen may learn that this threatening behavior actually works to get her what she wants and she may begin to use this behavior to get her needs met, even though that wasn't its initial intent. While you might be understandably angry when you think that your teen is using this behavior to get what she wants, it will help you respond less emotionally and more effectively when you can keep in mind that the original intent of the behavior was to manage her pain.

Understanding Suicidal Thoughts and Behaviors

Teens may become hopeless or depressed based on a negative event in their lives or may experience these feelings unrelated to a specific prompting event. Some teens feel as if a black cloud has always hovered over them, diminishing any pleasure in their lives; for others, this may be a new feeling. Teens who feel helpless to change how they feel and hopeless that their lives can improve may contemplate death as a way out of their misery.

Teens want desperately to end the pain that they feel is unrelenting and may feel that suicide is the only answer.

Understanding Self-Harming Behaviors

Self-harm is any emotionally driven, deliberate behavior that results in external or internal physical damage. Here are some of the reasons that a teen may self-harm:

- to regulate emotions; an attempt to manage the pain she's experiencing in the moment

- to punish herself

- to feel something other than numbness

- to reduce isolation and increase identification with a peer group

Some self-harming behaviors (such as cutting) result in the release of endorphins, which provide pleasure as an antidote to the pain being experienced by the teen. These behaviors continue because they relieve emotional pain immediately. It's easy to see why this behavior may be used over and over by a teen whose emotional pain is overwhelming.

Many teens self-harm in places where others won't observe it, such as on their stomach, thighs, buttocks, or other hidden areas. If you believe that your teen is self-harming for attention, the secrecy of the behavior may help you accept that the intent may be different than you originally thought.

The relief that the teen feels after self-harming can be immediate. *After* the teen has engaged in the behavior and reduced the intensity of her pain, she may then experience shame or disappointment in herself. Some teens begin to worry about scarring or about upsetting or disappointing people they care about or who care about them.

One of the goals of treatment is to help your teen develop awareness of the negative consequences of the behavior *prior* to engaging in the behavior so she can choose not to self-harm and thus feel less shame and self-disappointment. If your teen is in treatment, she can learn other behaviors that can relieve her pain, although not always with the same efficacy or efficiency. She can learn that using alternative, healthier behaviors will lessen immediate and long-term negative consequences and help her feel better about herself.

Parental Responses to Suicidal or Self-Harming Behaviors

Like other parents of teens or young adults with suicidal or self-harming behaviors, you may often question what you should do to keep your teen safe, how to respond when you find out that she has self-harmed, and how to validate her feelings in these situations. You may ask questions like these: "When I see evidence of self-harm, should I (1) talk to her about why she did this, (2) call her therapist, (3) check her room or put away all of my knives, (4) tell her how I feel about this behavior, (5) take away her activities or privileges, or (6) take her to a hospital?" There are no easy responses, no easy answers. Effective responses involve thinking and acting wisely and remaining focused on long- as well as short-term goals. We will discuss possible responses in this section through the vignette below:

> Ava, age fifteen, had been having increasing difficulty keeping up with her schoolwork. Then her boyfriend of three months broke up with her and she became very depressed. Her parents didn't want to upset her further, so they lessened their expectations and left her alone in her room a great deal of the time. Shortly after the breakup, they received a call from the school guidance counselor who told them that some other students reported they were worried when Ava mentioned that she wanted to die, and they were concerned about the scratches they noticed on her arms. When her parents asked her about her references to wanting to die, she laughed and said she was just joking. She didn't understand why her friends were upset or reported this. Her response to questions about the scratches was that

she had scratched her arms a few times with a paper clip and wasn't going to do it anymore. They scheduled an appointment with her pediatrician, who discovered that she had been cutting her thighs and stomach, with significant scarring, for some time. Her parents were confused about the behavior and felt guilty that they weren't aware of what she was doing. They began to question themselves and wondered what kind of parents didn't know about such significant behavior or about their daughter's now apparent distress. At the same time, Ava began to talk to them about how awful she has been feeling since the breakup with her boyfriend and how hopeless she feels about her life.

Parental Response to Suicide Threats or Behaviors

Whether the issue is chronic depression or situational depression, *any* talk about wanting to die, especially if there is a plan ("I feel like jumping out a window"; "I know where to get lots of pills that I can take"), must be taken seriously. You cannot assess whether or not your teen "means it," and you'll need to find ways to keep her safe *and* have her evaluated by a mental health professional. This may mean bringing your teen to her therapist, calling a mobile crisis team (if there's one available where you live), or taking her to a local emergency room for an evaluation.

It's also important, if there are concerns about a young person's safety, to make sure that she doesn't have immediate access to things she can use to kill herself (including knives or guns) and that medications (prescription or over the counter) that may be used to overdose are locked away. A teen's desire for privacy should not get in the way of protecting her if she has suicidal urges or intent. You can and should search her room, her backpack, or other places where she might be hiding the means to kill herself. If you're worried that your teen is more honest about her feelings with her friends on social media than she is with you directly, which may be the case, you may decide to read her social media *if* this information will help you keep her alive.

Providing Guidance When Your Teen Is Being Assessed

Teens may know how to control the outcome of an assessment and avoid treatment or hospitalization by telling the mental health evaluator "I didn't mean it" or "I'm safe now." If you, the parent, have feedback for the professional about past behaviors and history, recent unsafe behaviors, and/or what your teen is saying about wanting to die, you should provide this information, in clear, descriptive words and as calmly as possible, so that the mental health professional has a more thorough understanding on which to base treatment decisions.

A caveat about safety contracts. You may have heard from a mental health professional who is assessing your teen that she has signed a "safety contract" in which she has promised to be safe and to contact someone if she's thinking of killing herself. This kind of contract is *only* meaningful if it's between your teen and someone she respects. Teens may sign safety contracts in order to stay out of a hospital or to be able to do what they want. This doesn't mean that they've stopped thinking about suicide or won't act on the urge. Only trust those contracts that are between your teen and someone she cares about and would not want to disappoint. And, dialectically, you may also need to accept that this contract will not always work either. If a teen is overwhelmed by a sense of misery and pain, no contract may be able to stop the behavior that she thinks will end that pain.

Parental Response to Self-Harm

If your teen is self-harming, your most important role is to try to provide as much safety as possible. That might mean checking her room and removing access to knives, pills, and other means of self-harm, as necessary. Self-harming behavior can accidentally be lethal; you need to ensure that there is nothing readily available that a depressed, impulsive teen could use which unintentionally might result in significant damage or death.

Sometimes creating a safer environment is difficult. You and other family members might be inconvenienced when kitchen knives are stored elsewhere or when all pills are locked up. You might be ambivalent about creating an environment that doesn't feel typical or desirable to you. Remember that you want to do everything you can to protect your teen until she's able to maintain her own safety.

The Limits of Providing Safety

You may be aware of the dialectic that you can do everything you can to create a safe environment and still your teen might find ways to self-harm if she wants to. Ava's parents might take away all the knives in the house, and she might still harm herself with a paper clip, staple, or her own fingernails. You have to do the best you can to keep your teen safe *and* accept that there are limits to these measures; your teen will ultimately be the one to decide to change her own behavior and become safer.

Safety and Privacy

You may be wondering about the apparent conflict of maintaining safety while also respecting your teen's right to privacy and not wanting to betray her. Because safety is the most important priority, you may need to search your teen's room without permission. If you're concerned that she may become angry or aggressive while you're searching, you can do it when she's not home. This is not an opportunity to snoop, only to remove anything that the teen can use to self-harm. It's both an attempt at maintaining safety and a message to your child that you care about her and about keeping her safe. If your teen becomes angry at what she sees as a betrayal, validate her feelings and let her know that your priority is safety, not privacy.

If you think the best way to know about your teen's safety is to read her texts or online posts, do so as long as the information is used only to keep her safe, not to blame or accuse. If you won't actually use the information to keep her safe because you don't want her to know you're following her, all your monitoring does is cause you anxiety and betray your teen. Think about your reasons for doing this and assess the pros and cons. If it helps you keep your teen safe, continue to do it; if it only causes you more anxiety, don't do it, and do whatever else you can to be vigilant and monitor your teen's behaviors without invading her privacy.

Validation

If your teen is suicidal or self-harming, you may feel frustration and anger at her secrecy or behaviors, confused about why she's doing this to herself, and fear that she might seriously harm or kill herself. It's even harder and more confusing when your teen or young adult masks her pain and covers up how she feels or when it isn't clear what might be causing her distress. All of your emotions make it harder to remember that these behaviors are caused by your teen's distress and make it harder to validate her.

Acknowledge Your Own Feelings

Parents, like Ava's, who find out that their teen is having suicidal thoughts or self-harming feel any number of emotions as they enter this uncharted territory. It makes sense that you would feel scared that your teen might seriously harm herself or actually kill herself. Fear and anxiety become the defining emotions for parents in this situation. Other feelings are also understandable:

- fear and worry about what might happen

- desperation, and sometimes helplessness, about stopping your teen's behavior and making her feel better

- anger that your teen is behaving in such a dangerous way

- confusion about why your teen is feeling so desperate and why she behaves as she does

- embarrassment and shame that your teen is having problems, and even more shame that you weren't aware of them

- isolation and fear that your friends and family won't understand

- guilt that you might have done something to cause this

- sadness that your teen is in so much pain

You have to remember that you, too, are doing the best you can. It's invaluable for you to share your feelings with your partner or coparent and with other parents so that you can manage your own emotions effectively. You may find it helpful to talk to your own parent coach or therapist so that you can receive support and validation for your feelings. Sadly, you may feel so embarrassed by, and ashamed of, your teen's desire to die or self-harm that you isolate yourself from helpful activities and supports when you need them most. Reaching out to those you trust may help you manage your own emotions more effectively.

Acknowledge What's Real to Your Teen

Parents often hope the issues that teens face are momentary problems that will resolve themselves with time—and that may well be the case with many teens. However, teens who have intense emotions often think that their difficult situations are unending; feel their pain more acutely than their friends, parents, or anyone else who has more typical emotions; and sometimes do not see ways out of their situations. They contemplate suicide or self-harm as a way out or to feel better immediately, and this behavior is effective in mitigating the pain for the moment.

Ava's parents might not have realized the degree to which her pain felt unmanageable. If her parents try to offer their support and provide encouragement with comments like "Maybe it's for the best that your boyfriend left" or "There will be other boyfriends" or "We're sure these feelings will pass," she will likely experience these comments as invalidating and further proof that nobody can understand the pain she feels.

Validation of teens who think about suicide or self-harm focuses on the pain, disappointment, hopelessness, and misery the teen is feeling. It's important to acknowledge the desperation your teen feels to get rid of her misery. At the same time, it's not effective to validate or accept *behavior* that isn't healthy or safe. *Validation is always about accepting emotions and not about approving of behaviors.* Ava's parents can genuinely acknowledge (1) how sad she has been feeling and how lonely she must have felt not sharing that sadness, (2) how painful it must have been for her when she thought that nobody would understand, (3) that she might be angry at her

119

friends for telling the counselor about her, and (4) how hopeless she must be feeling to be thinking that she might not want to live. You can validate your teen's feelings of pain, despair, disappointment, or anger while making it clear that you will continue to do all you can to help her maintain safe behaviors.

Validate Painful Emotions

Ava's parents will need to find a way to validate Ava's sadness that will feel genuine to her. She might initially reject their attempts at validation if they say they "understand" or they "get it" and Ava has no evidence that they do. Here are some ways that Ava's parents might validate her pain prior to, and with the hope of minimizing, any future suicide attempts or self-harm:

- They could listen with their full attention when she talks about feeling sad, without trying to help her get rid of the sadness.

- They could acknowledge her pain by saying, "We can't even imagine how awful this must feel to you."

- They might say, "Now we get how miserable you felt when you broke up with your boyfriend."

- They could tell Ava, "We're here for you whenever you want us to be. How can we help?"

Using Reinforcers Strategically

When Ava's parents find out that she's thinking about suicide or self-harming, they may want to give her much more attention, talk to her about her unsafe thoughts or behaviors, or let her do whatever she wants so that she'll feel better. It's easy to see how self-harming behaviors may inadvertently be reinforced by parental attention and concern when parents want to do all they can to be vigilant around their teen's safety, help minimize her misery, and provide support. And it's easy to be so focused on unsafe behaviors that you don't notice when your teen is sharing her day with you, talking to her friends on the phone, doing her homework, spending time with the family, or doing other typical or healthy behaviors. These healthy behaviors may be taken for granted and go unnoticed or unattended to. And yet it's very important and beneficial when you notice, acknowledge, and reinforce healthy behaviors; your teen realizes that she'll receive attention and positive feedback for her healthy behaviors, and these may in turn increase.

Managing the Desire to Attend to Self-Harm

When Ava's parents find out that she's self-harming, they want to see all the scars and they ask her continuously if she's being safe. All of this attention to self-harm may actually reinforce the behavior. Therefore, parents whose children are in treatment are often encouraged not to ask about this behavior and not to attend to it. While you do need to make sure that your teen doesn't need medical attention, after this assessment, it's most effective for you not to give the self-harm any additional attention, even if this is very difficult for you. If your teen has a therapist or counselor—and it's critical in these situations that she has professional help—let the mental health professional know that you've noticed self-harm. You'll be more effective when you're attentive to healthy behaviors and let mental health professionals attend to the self-harming behaviors.

Only the Teen Can Lessen Her Misery

When Ava's parents realize how miserable their daughter is, they want to give her whatever privileges she wants, even allowing her to participate in activities she previously was not able to, in an attempt to help her feel better and have some pleasure in her life. Ava may find, for example, that she can now go out even if her homework isn't done. In an attempt to help her feel better, it's understandable that parents might change how they parent when they find out that their daughter is so unhappy.

This change in parenting style inadvertently reinforces Ava's misery as she sees that sometimes, she can get more privileges when she's sad than when she isn't. Parents need to think wisely about how they respond when their teen is suicidal or self-harming. Privileges and freedoms still need to be earned by healthy behaviors. While it may be difficult to refuse requests from a teen who is so miserable, you can validate her disappointment while reminding yourself that teens do need structure and limits in order to develop into healthy adults.

Your teen will not become happier in the long run if you give her all the privileges she wants. You can show your love, support, and caring for your teen when you continue to provide structure, reinforce her healthy choices, and support her efforts toward change. You'll parent more effectively when you recognize and accept that you cannot make your teen happy; only she can do that for herself. Your teen's misery won't end because she can do things that she thinks will make her happy. She can help herself get out of her misery only through the hard work of learning how to think differently about her circumstances and her life and making changes in how she behaves when she is in emotional distress or pain.

Responding to Threats

Teens whose self-harming behaviors, or even their misery and thoughts about dying, have been inadvertently reinforced by parents may begin to threaten their parents in order to get what they want. Parents report teens who say, "If you don't let me go to the party, I'll slit my wrists" or "If I can't see my friends tonight, you may not see me in the morning." And parents, who know that these threats can be realized, may give in to keep their teens from harming themselves, thereby reinforcing threatening behaviors. As hard as it might be, you should not give a teen what she wants after she has threatened suicide or self-harm. Validate her feelings and then continue to observe the limit that has been set, regardless of an increase in threats. Though the behavior may increase initially, this is the only way to diminish or eventually end threatening behaviors.

At the same time, *threatening behaviors cannot be ignored*. You will need to maintain your vigilance without direct attention so as to make sure your teen is as safe as possible. If you are concerned about the possibility that your teen will do serious harm, have her evaluated by a mental health professional.

Taking your child for an evaluation is a natural consequence when a teen or young adult is threatening harm. If your teen is significantly harming herself, she may be hospitalized until she can maintain her safety. If she's using the threat to get her needs met, she'll learn that the threats don't have the intended effect. This response helps you feel more confident that you're keeping your teen safe without reinforcing her threats. If you're worried that this response may cause your teen to be more secretive, you'll appreciate knowing this tends not to be the case. It actually provides the opportunity for your teen to learn to use healthier ways to express herself and get her needs met.

A caveat for parents is that some teens may find it reinforcing to get attention from mental health professionals, and you may hesitate to take her there if she gets the attention she wants as a result. However, if there is any question about safety, whether it encourages or discourages future threats, an assessment will still be necessary.

Responding to Depressed Behavior Whether or Not There Is Self-Harm

You may become very worried, concerned, or fearful when your teen is withdrawn, has given up activities that she used to enjoy, loses connections with or has few friends, and is not completing the basic requirements of life (such as showering or doing chores or homework). You may feel bewildered about what to do, how many expectations to have, how much you should let go, and how much you should encourage or push your teen into typical activities. The knowledge that your teen is self-harming or thinking of suicide creates even more fear than less dangerous, although still problematic, behaviors.

Prioritize Your Concerns

When a teen is depressed or unsafe, you'll want to focus on helping her to remain safe and do the work required to become less depressed. This might mean letting go of other expectations in the short run. While it may appear to you that your teen is not doing anything, the effort it requires to stay safe and alive, despite emotional misery, cannot be minimized and may take all the energy your teen has, leaving little for anything else. Getting the support and treatment she needs to learn how to manage her painful emotions will be a priority for you.

If your teen is genuinely struggling and seems unmotivated even to live, it's hard for her to concentrate on anything else. You may find that you have to readjust your expectations to accommodate your teen's emotional difficulties. This does not mean that your teen should be treated as fragile. You can continue to have some expectations, continue to ask the teen to do as much as she is able to, *and* be ready to accept that she may be doing the best she can even if she seems to be doing very little. As she gets healthier, increase your expectations commensurately.

Create a Soothing, Pleasurable Environment

Teens who have intensely sad emotions may be more reactive in environments where there is anger and tension. Your teen may be reacting to your fears, concerns, and anxieties as much as you're reacting to hers. Teens pick up on nonverbal cues and know when you're distressed. In Ava's case, Ava's parents will have to manage their emotional reactivity to her behaviors by taking care of themselves and their needs. This will enable them to remain calm when they're interacting with her.

As much as possible, create an environment that allows your teen to engage in activities that she may enjoy. Ava's parents had been giving her space and time alone and began to realize that this might not have been so helpful. You may realize that your teen communicates while watching a favorite TV show or that she laughs when she joins the family to watch a movie, making these activities that connect her with her family and keep her safe. Going out for ice cream or a coffee is another way that you can engage your teen in a way that she enjoys. Encourage these healthy behaviors. While your teen may feel anxious in large groups (even at family gatherings), she may be willing to share activities with a parent, a relative, or a close friend. As much as possible, create a calming, soothing, pleasurable home environment that might help your teen reconnect with life.

Acceptance

Parents who have teens who self-harm or are suicidal need to mourn the teen they expected in order to accept the teen they have. All parents want their kids to lead healthy lives in which they enjoy friends and activities, go to school, meet ever-growing challenges, and maximize their potential for success. It's hard to acknowledge that these expectations may not be met, at least not in the short run. The journey of your teen may be very different than what you anticipated or hoped for her. It's only slowly, over time, that you may come to accept that your teen's life may always be somewhat painful and difficult, at some times more than others. The more you accept this, the better able you will be to help your teen lead the life that works for her. The path and the eventual destination may be different, although the teen who stays alive through these turbulent years can still have the life she wants to live.

Ava's parents will begin to recognize that their daughter needs help to learn how to manage her emotions in safer ways. As a family, they may have to do some work to learn how to express emotions in healthy ways and listen to each other. They all may have to change some of the ways in which they interact and the expectations they have of each other. Ava's parents may have to accept that in order to help Ava move forward, they may have to allow for some detours along the way.

Summary

In this chapter, we provided you with ways to understand why some teens or young adults self-harm or become suicidal. We acknowledged the feelings you experience as you navigate your way through unexpected situations. We provided you with specific strategies you can use in responding to unsafe behaviors. We discussed the importance of prioritizing expectations and accepting that the life of a teen who is self-harming may be different than what you had expected.

Key Points:

- Safety has to be a priority if a teen is suicidal or self-harming.

- Self-harming is serious and can result in death.

- Self-harming may be reinforced by the pain relief it provides, the social connection that may result, and by the way parents respond to it.

- Parents can validate the pain that underlies self-harming behavior without validating the behavior itself.

- It's most effective for parents to focus their attention and interactions on behaviors that are healthy.

- Treatment is a priority for a teen who self-harms or is suicidal.

- Parents need to do all they can to create a safe environment while accepting that only the teen can decide to give up self-harming or suicidal behavior and focus on creating the life she wants.

Chapter 6

Disruptive, Risky, and Substance-Abusing Behaviors

This chapter will be relevant to you if your teen or young adult has any of the following behaviors: substance abuse, aggression, verbal and physical abuse, sexual promiscuity, illegal behaviors, lying and stealing, risk taking online or in person.

Some teens display their emotional distress with aggression, lying, stealing, or refusing to respond to limits or expectations. Other teens may take dangerous risks or put themselves in situations in which they may be harmed (being with strangers while using drugs and alcohol, meeting people for hookups that they've never met face-to-face, and so on). Other teens may use substances in their attempts to feel better or to be comfortable in social situations. Some teens become verbally abusive to or even steal from family members. If your teen or young adult has any of these behaviors, you, like other parents in similar situations, probably experience tremendous confusion, frustration, disappointment, anger, and fear. You know you have tried to raise your child to behave more responsibly and are scared of the harm that your teen may cause to himself or others. In addition, you may be embarrassed or ashamed when your teen gets in trouble or becomes involved with the police or courts because of dangerous or illegal behaviors.

In this chapter, we will help you understand these behaviors. We will also teach you ways to respond most effectively when your teen with intense emotions displays disruptive, risky, or substance-abusing behaviors.

Understanding Disruptive, Risky, and Substance-Abusing Behaviors

How do you begin to understand why your teen lies to or steals from you, or why he creates fear in your home with his aggressive and violent behaviors? What can you do when he puts himself into risky or dangerous situations? Parents report incredible bewilderment, consternation, and disappointment when they have to lock their bedroom door or hide their money because they cannot trust their teen not to take things that aren't his. Like other parents, you may be dismayed and shocked by your teen's verbal or physical abuse. Or, if you have always been a law-abiding citizen, you may find yourself thrust into a legal system to help your teen whose behaviors are inexplicable to you.

While you may never truly understand how your teen can behave in these ways, you will become less angry when you see these behaviors through the prism of understanding that your teen's brain is highly sensitive to emotional situations rather than the belief that your teen has antisocial behavior, and when you recognize that there is hope for behavior change rather than expect a lifetime of illegal or dangerous behaviors. While experiencing these behaviors may always be painful and difficult, understanding may help you accept your teen, which can then enable you to find more effective ways to help him.

Aggressive and Dangerous Behaviors

Aggressive and dangerous behaviors can largely be understood within the context of pain, boredom, and impulsivity. These behaviors are driven by a complex mix of factors:

- **Outward expression of emotional pain.** For some teens, feeling their emotions very intensely leads to behavior that appears to be out of control; they express their emotional pain outwardly, toward others, by acting aggressively or even violently.

- **Frustrated goals or feeling "stuck."** Some teens are easily upset when they're stopped from pursuing their goals and may impulsively respond with aggression. Since the aggressive behaviors often result in what they want, the behaviors continue. Other teens may become frustrated when they "get stuck" and don't see alternate ways of understanding and responding to events. This frustration may lead to angry outbursts, which relieve their discomfort. Some teens then experience shame about their own behavior. This may lead to further emotional distress, which then leads to additional problematic behaviors. The satisfaction associated with expressing anger helps young people momentarily feel better, and as a result, angry outbursts become more likely the next time they're emotionally triggered.

- **Need for stimulation and excitement.** Other teens may find that the typical experiences of adolescent life are not enough to keep them stimulated; they may be intolerant of boredom and have a strong desire to feel more excitement, which leads to risk-taking behavior. The risky, dangerous behavior enables the teen to feel more alive or energized. The positive feelings that result and the fact that the behavior may be valued by the peer group lead to even more risk-taking behaviors. Over time, the teen may need to heighten the level of risk in order to feel better, and the behaviors may then become even more dangerous.

- **Impulsivity and inability to effectively manage emotions.** For most teens who act in aggressive and dangerous ways, impulsivity is also a significant factor. Usually, these teens are not skilled at managing their emotions effectively. When they become upset, they impulsively react with behaviors that, while upsetting to parents, may actually get them what they want more times than not.

After aggressive or dangerous behaviors, there may be a period of calm in which your teen begins to feel remorse for his behaviors and feels bad about the disruption he causes in the family. He may, at this time, genuinely apologize for his behaviors and say he will change them. And yet the pattern repeats itself. You are caught between wanting to believe the apology and hoping that your teen will change and ongoing hopelessness, fear, frustration, and anger when the behaviors continue.

If your teen apologizes, you may question the sincerity of his apology when the behaviors continue over time. However, it's possible that at the time your teen apologizes, he is genuinely remorseful. He generally doesn't want to cause you emotional grief and doesn't want to be involved in legal proceedings that might result from his behavior. Remember that the emotional discomfort your teen feels is hard for him to manage, and until he learns more skillful behavior, he'll continue to respond in the ways that bring him immediate, albeit brief, relief. The cycle continues because in the moment of emotional pain, he's less aware of long-term consequences, and in the short run, he may get (1) his needs met, (2) peer approval, and/or (3) relief from his discomfort.

Substance-Abusing Behaviors

Young people who experience emotional distress, anxiety, depression, or misery might turn to substances to numb the pain, relieve discomfort and distress, lessen inhibitions, and enable themselves to engage more comfortably in social activities while feeling more accepted by their peers. They may find that substances help them feel better. Or they may find their life so understimulating that they seek out the extreme and unusual experiences associated with alcohol and drug intoxication. The result of using substances is immediately reinforcing (by lessening stress and discomfort and helping the teen to feel better) and thus continues to override any concerns about possible consequences. It's usually more acceptable among your teen's friends to be using substances than to be seen as having emotional problems. It's also more acceptable to him to be using substances than to be taking psychiatric drugs to manage his anxiety or other emotional difficulties.

Many teens, even those in treatment, want to continue their sub-stance use; they don't want to give up what, in the short run, is working so well for them. They may recognize the consequences—that they have fewer freedoms, that their parents are generally angry at them, or that they may not be able to complete their schoolwork or other responsibilities—and yet they know that the way they feel on substances is much better than how they feel when they're not using substances. For the teen, the positive consequences outweigh the negative consequences.

Your teen's desire to maintain a behavior that you see as disruptive to his life is maddening. Eventually, it's important for your teen to recognize—with your help and the help of any treatment providers—that he can have a satisfying and fulfilling life worth living even, and in fact, especially, if he's not using substances.

Lying and Stealing

You may feel stumped if your teen lies to you or steals from you or others. It's very distressing and difficult to live in a family where there's little trust in one member. As incredulous as it seems to you that your teen denies behavior that only he could have done, you may find it helps to understand that some people who react to the world emotionally may distort the facts of a situation to match their emotions (Linehan 1993a). Your teen's chief focus will be getting his needs met, and he'll do what he needs to do or say what he needs to say to meet his needs in the moment, without thinking about potential consequences. Ultimately, lying and stealing often provide more consistent positive reinforcement for young people than occasional consequences take away. For your teen, the bene-fits of stealing and having the things he wants or money to spend on what-ever he desires will often outweigh any consequences that you may occasionally impose on those rare instances when he's caught.

Young people may feel remorse and a genuine desire to act in a more trustworthy way at times when they're more in control of their emotions and behaviors. While your teen may realize that he'll get more privileges and freedoms when you trust him, the behavior itself is so immediately reinforcing that it's hard for him to give it up. When his emotions are spiraling out of control, he may act impulsively to get what he wants, without regard to the consequences to himself or others.

Your teen may also begin to adopt the identity of a rebel, justifying his behaviors as a necessary response to an unfair world, and he may feel supported by friends. The societal response—involvement with the police, court system, and so on—might further marginalize your teen. He may then become even more entrenched in a pattern of behaviors that lead to more and more trouble. To change this pattern, he will need to learn that trustworthy behaviors can have their own reward and will enable him to have the kind of life he wants to have.

Risky Relationships

Teens or young adults who experience intense and overwhelming emotions may feel empty, lonely, or isolated. Sometimes their emotional reactions and disruptive or aggressive behaviors have distanced them from others in their peer group. Without skills to manage moods or social interactions effectively, and in order to meet their basic human need to connect, they may seek out others like themselves or strangers (either virtually, through social media, or face-to-face) who will meet their needs in the moment. They may not address the potential dangers or worry about the negative consequences until well after the negative consequences have occurred. They may take enormous risks because their desire to connect and to lessen their sense of emptiness overrides their inhibitions or concerns for their safety in the moment.

Your teen may have found that the need for connection can be met through sexual promiscuity and ongoing sexual encounters with individuals who are met online or elsewhere. The perception of real intimacy and closeness is immediately reinforcing for the teen who's looking for connection and discovering that sexuality has value to others. Some teens find this behavior socially acceptable, which further reinforces it for the teen who has intense emotions. Even teens who have been harmed in these situations may return to them again and again. They may deny the potential risks, letting their emotions override their reason or feeling that the risk is worth what they experience.

Some teens experience guilt, shame, and remorse after being in risky or sexually promiscuous interactions, and these feelings can be overwhelming, leading to even more risky behavior in an attempt to manage these uncomfortable feelings. At times, they may recognize the potential consequences as well as how detrimental this behavior is to their self-respect and self-esteem. In the long run, they may recognize that the behavior is troubling and may actually have more negative consequences than they originally thought.

Despite the potential for shame and guilt, your teen, even when in treatment, may find the behavior itself so reinforcing that it's hard to give it up. Your teen may feel most "alive" and "normal" when involved in risky or potentially dangerous situations. Despite the fact that your teen may act in ways that are inconsistent with your values, the intense and overwhelming emotions continue to lead to dangerous ways of responding to emotional distress. When your teen finds healthier ways to meet the need for connection and excitement, a life filled with more self-esteem and less shame will develop.

Parental Responses to Disruptive, Risky, and Substance-Abusing Behaviors

If your teen or young adult behaves in ways that disrupt your family, abuses substances, or acts in illegal or what you consider shameful or immoral ways, you, like other parents, may often vacillate between anger at these behaviors and fear for your teen. You may also feel bewildered about how to respond, fearful about possible aggressive reactions from your teen, and helpless because there seems to be so little you can do to change these behaviors.

Here are some of the questions parents like you ask when confronted by these behaviors:

- "How do I continue to live with my child when I have to lock away my valuables?"

- "Do I continue to let him live at home, and where would he go if we kicked him out?"

- "How do I set limits when his reaction can be so violent?"

- "How do I make sure that my other children are safe and not disrupted or scared by these behaviors?"

- "Are there any consequences that will really matter?"

- "Do we invade his privacy by searching his room or reading his social media accounts?"

- "Do we call the police or turn him in? What would happen to him if we did this?"

- "Do we help him if he gets into legal difficulties?"

- "Do we address the behaviors through drug rehab or therapy for emotional difficulties?"

- "How do we help our teen make safe choices about sexual behavior?"

These are very difficult questions, and the answers are not always clear and certainly not easy to find. There may actually be different answers at different times and in different circumstances. We provide some answers to these questions through a discussion of the vignette below:

Eric's parents have been struggling to respond effectively to his behavior. He was arrested for marijuana possession a year ago and completed the requirements of the juvenile services program he was referred to. He has resumed using marijuana and has not responded to limits his parents set around it. He often leaves the house to take walks at night, despite the fact that they've asked him not to do this. While he denies he's using, they smell marijuana when he returns. He has also taken money from them, and they have fallen into a pattern of looking the other way so as not to create more conflict in the family.

This uneasy truce was shattered when they learned that Eric had used a fraudulently obtained credit card to have drug paraphernalia shipped to a neighbor's house while the neighbors were away on vacation. Now the police are involved again, and Eric's parents don't know what to do. Whenever they try to address these issues with Eric, he gets angry, verbally abusive, aggressive, and refuses to talk about it. They're afraid of him and afraid for him.

Validation

You may question how you can validate a teen who behaves aggressively, steals from you, or engages in risky behaviors that you cannot condone. It's important to remember that you're *not* validating the behavior and you don't have to like that behavior, support it, or agree with it. The task is to understand and validate the underlying emotional components that drive the behavior, components like those we discussed in the previous section. When you validate, you genuinely acknowledge the pain and discomfort your teen feels.

Acknowledge Your Own Emotions

It's important for you to manage your own very understandable and discomforting emotions so that you can validate and address your teen in the most effective way possible. When your teen is so disruptive to everyone in the family, you might experience overwhelming anger. You struggle to accept or understand your teen when his behavior is contradictory to your moral values. And there are often other feelings that come and go as well. As can be seen in this chapter's vignette, Eric's parents experience a variety of complex, sometimes contradictory, emotions:

- anger and frustration at their son who doesn't follow their expectations and who sometimes behaves in verbally abusive, aggressive, or illegal ways

- embarrassment that their child has legal difficulties

- bewilderment that the boy they raised can behave in ways that are so contradictory to their own values

- helpless to do anything to change the situation or to help their son

- dismay and disappointment that they can't trust their own child

- anxiety about what might happen to him

- confusion about balancing the desire to protect him from the consequences of his behavior while also wanting him to learn from the natural consequences

You may find that a prominent feeling for you is fear; you may be so afraid of a dangerous, aggressive, or unsafe response from your teen that you may hesitate to ask anything of him or set any limit. Or you may be so afraid of these consequences that you may want to look the other way. While these reactions are understandable, you don't parent as effectively when you're fearful. To be effective as a parent, acknowledge your fears and find ways to manage them while also maintaining safety in your home.

You cannot deny your feelings and hope that they will go away. Making wise decisions will mean that you understand your emotions at the same time that you try to understand the feelings of your teen. Eric's parents may be too embarrassed to discuss these issues with others, and, because of that, they may feel isolated. However, talking with others will help, especially those who can provide some validation for their feelings. Eric's parents may also find that other parents have faced similar situations in the past and may be able to provide helpful advice as well as validation. If you face a situation like Eric's parents, keeping these issues a secret means that you may become overwhelmed by your own painful emotions and be unable to parent as effectively as necessary.

Acknowledge What's Real to Your Teen

You may be able to accept why your teen abuses substances based on understanding that he is trying to manage intense emotions and using drugs helps him do this. What's more difficult to accept or understand is how your own child, who you raised with certain values, can lie to and steal from you or others or participate in illegal, immoral, or sexually risky activities. It's understandable that you don't know what you can possibly validate.

Search nonjudgmentally for what's valid to your teen and what he might be experiencing. In the vignette, Eric's parents might be able to acknowledge that (1) Eric really feels he needs marijuana in order to manage his emotions, (2) he hasn't mastered effective skills for managing his emotions, (3) his behaviors are driven by his emotional and social needs, which make it hard for him to think beyond his immediate desire for the pleasure he gets from using marijuana, (4) his emotions and use of marijuana interfere with his learning how to cope and applying this learning to new situations, (5) he cannot think through the longer-term consequences when he's focused on his immediate need, and (6) he may feel shame and guilt when he's confronted with his behaviors, emotions that are also hard for him to tolerate and which may lead to more problematic behaviors and anger.

Here are some of the comments that Eric's parents might make—gently, calmly, and nonjudgmentally:

- "We know you like marijuana and that you're frustrated when you can't use it and we don't allow it."

- "We know that you're angry with us."

- "We get that you don't want to talk about this situation."

- "It's hard for you—and for us—that there's no trust between us."

Understanding why your teen behaves in this way doesn't mean that you excuse the behaviors or accept them. It only helps you to respond more wisely, and to calm your own and your teen's emotional intensity so that problem solving can occur. Expressing anger toward your teen when his intense emotions are causing his behaviors to escalate dangerously will likely lead to more increased tension and conflict and the possibility of aggression in your home. Validation helps to lessen the intensity in these situations.

Expectations and Limits

Structure and rules are important to teens, both in the present and for their future; they'll always live in a world that asks for some conformity to rules. Develop a structure for your teen that includes rules, expectations, and limits, even if your teen doesn't initially obey them. Young people need to know the boundaries, even if they're breaking them. There are always behaviors that you cannot reasonably control, *and* it's still important to let your teen know clearly and without question what behaviors are expected, allowed, or not allowed in your home. You can also clearly state your concerns about risky behaviors and their consequences.

This is the dialectic: you know your teen may ignore rules or limits while also recognizing that he needs to know what those limits and expectations are. You may find that you have to accept things or make compromises that may feel somewhat uncomfortable to you. For example, you may have to accept that your teen uses marijuana outside of the home; and at the same time, you don't have to give him permission, like it, or permit its use anywhere in or around your home. As difficult as it is, you'll find that you're parenting most effectively when you don't battle with your teen about what you cannot control, and at the same time, can state your views clearly and back them up with consequences and rewards when possible.

Prioritizing Expectations and Limits

If your teen acts disruptively or displays risky behaviors, you have to choose carefully when to set and enforce limits and what expectations to have. Above all, as parents, you want to create emotional and physical safety in your home—for yourselves, your other children, and your teen. You may need to accept, with great difficulty, that a teen with disruptive, aggressive, risky, or substance-abusing behaviors may not be able or willing to participate in the family in the way you would like. Creating power struggles by demanding behaviors that your teen refuses to do often leads to more aggression.

Prioritize what's most important and what will create the safest environment for everyone. You may prioritize that your teen refrain from (1) physical aggression in your home, (2) bringing strangers into your home, (3) talking about risky sexual activities at home or with younger siblings, (4) having or using substances or alcohol in the house, or (5) emotionally or physically abusing members of the family. Develop your priorities by keeping in mind the bigger picture of emotional and physical safety for all members of your family. When you're thinking wisely, you will see that these issues are more important than whether or not the teen is on the computer too much or not joining the family for activities.

Eric does not have life-threatening behaviors, and so his parents will prioritize their concerns in this order: (1) Eric's aggression in the home because it's a safety issue, (2) getting Eric into treatment, (3) responding effectively to his continuing use of marijuana, and (4) responding effectively to his legal issues. His verbal aggression may be a lower priority, even though it's very disruptive to all family members. Other parents may prioritize the legal issues over the marijuana use. These decisions, while based on an understanding about the importance of safety and treatment, will also depend on parental values and the ways in which behaviors affect the family in the moment.

In addition, limits around phone and/or computer use should take into account whether or not the teen is using them in a safe manner. Visiting sites that trigger or promote self-harm, using phones to set up drug deals or sexual encounters with strangers, or buying things using stolen credit cards might necessitate taking away the phone and/or computer or strictly limiting their use. Your priority is to maintain as much safety as you can for your teen as well as the rest of your family, despite his desire to do whatever he chooses and your recognition that your actual ability to control your teen is very limited.

Responding to Theft at Home

It may be hard for you to imagine or accept, as it was for Eric's parents, that your teen might actually steal from you. You may be understandably upset and angry that you have to live with a lack of trust that necessitates locking bedroom doors or hiding valuables. And yet sometimes this is the only way that you can prevent further theft until your teen begins to acknowledge consequences and is willing and able to change his behaviors. The compromise here, paradoxically, is that you'll live in a locked environment that may be uncomfortable in order to provide a safe environment for your teen to live in, which provides you with some comfort.

Eric's parents (1) put locks on the doors to their private spaces and keep their valuables and their money locked there, (2) don't allow Eric to use their credit cards, (3) search his room for illegal substances and take away anything they find, and (4) monitor his computer use to make sure he's not using it to make illegal purchases.

Issues of Privacy

Teens don't want to have their private space (their bedroom, their computer) intruded upon by parents who may be looking for illegal substances or ensuring that they're safe on the Internet. Room searches may cause teens to become even more emotionally and behaviorally out of control. And still you can (and probably should) search your teen's space if you think that there are illegal substances in your home (which includes alcohol, since your teen is under the legal drinking age) and you can confiscate what you find. Likewise, Internet access can be limited or closely monitored if it's being used unsafely.

If you're concerned that your teen will become aggressive if he sees you searching his room, it may be safer for you to search his room when he's not home. That way he will not become aggressive toward you during the search. You can let your teen know that you always have the option of searching his room or reading his texts or postings, and that his safety will always be most important to you. Keeping your teen safe (even if he doesn't agree that what he's doing can be harmful) is more important than privacy and confidentiality, and you can make your decisions keeping that in mind.

Using Rewards and Punishment/Negative Consequences Strategically

If your teen does not follow rules and/or breaks the law, you may often feel frustrated by your inability to develop any control over his behaviors.

Typical rewards don't work because the teen takes whatever he wants without regard to the consequences. Punishment seems ineffective when the teen refuses to obey any limits that are set or any negative consequences that are implemented. You may wonder why your teen doesn't learn from experience and why he continues these behaviors despite the negative consequences they incur.

Rewards

Reward is a very powerful motivator, and it is the most effective parent response for changing behavior. It may be hard to find rewards for your teen, so you can use your own connectedness, your own warmth, anything you might buy for him, money, or any privileges you might give him as rewards. Reward any small or incremental change *every* time. Consistently notice and acknowledge positive behaviors, even in the midst of chaotic times. If your teen comes home by curfew, you may extend his curfew. If he manages his anger by leaving the room and settling down, offer to take him to do something he likes to do. In the case of Eric, his parents may begin to put money into an account for him when he follows any rule or meets any expectation without becoming angry. While it's challenging to find and reward positive behaviors when so much else may be going poorly, this approach gets results and leads to positive behavior change.

Trust

When your teen has behaved in ways that have broken your trust, he may not think that his behaviors should affect his privileges. You'll probably have to point out to him that his behaviors have certain consequences that include (1) not believing him when he tells you something, so you may not allow certain activities, (2) not giving him your credit card to use for something he wants even if he says he'll give it back to you, (3) not giving him any cash for fear he'll use it to buy drugs, and (4) not giving him the privacy he demands.

Once trust is broken, it has to be *earned* back. You can tell your teen what he needs to do that will instill trust, such as (1) following the rules and meeting expectations, (2) coming in when he's supposed to, (3) not using drugs in the home, (4) being where he says he is, and (5) letting you see that he's using his phone and computer safely. As he begins to meet your expectations, you might increase his privileges so that he can go out with friends, use his computer more, and, possibly, have access to your credit card when necessary. Trust breeds trust. It should not be given back unless and until it is earned.

Negative Consequences

As we mentioned earlier, you may often feel that there's little you can do that will have an effect on the behaviors of your teen. Yet you probably don't realize how much you do that is taken for granted by your teen; withdrawing some of what you do for him may, in fact, be an effective consequence. You might ask yourself how much you do for him—how often you drive him to activities or to friends' houses or whether you make sure that he has access to foods or other special products in your home that are bought especially for him. You might also notice how often you pay for things he wants to do (such as movies or concerts) or clothes he says he needs. If your teen is old enough to drive, does he have access to your car? If he has his own car, who pays for it? Who pays for gas? Who pays for insurance? When is he allowed to use it?

You actually do many more things for your teen than you realize. You may feel some of these things are done because it's your responsibility; others are done in an attempt to help your teen feel better. You, like most parents, want to take care of your teen regardless of his behaviors—and yet you can meet your basic responsibilities without doing anything extra or special for him. For example, you can stop doing things for him, taking him places, or giving him money or access to his car. As he begins to behave in more trustworthy, respectful, and less aggressive ways, you'll do more for him and give him more access to the privileges that he wants.

Negative consequences, even if they include not doing for your teen what you used to do for him, are difficult to implement. You may feel what parents often feel: (1) how hard it is to deny a teen who may become aggressive, (2) wanting to pay for gas to enable your teen to get places he needs to go to even if he goes elsewhere, (3) wanting to continue to help your teen do things he enjoys, or (4) wanting him to have some spending money so he doesn't steal or borrow it from others. Think wisely about what's most effective for your teen in the long run and make the hard choices about how much to continue to do for a teen who's disruptive or engaging in illegal activities.

It might be helpful to find a middle path, such as giving your teen spending or gas money in the form of a gift card specific to a store or gas station so that it cannot be used for drugs (although gift cards are often sold for cash). You can monitor his activities in the car through a GPS system so he can use the car for certain, prearranged activities. In these situations, he can earn more trust when he observes your limits and rules. At the same time, you do want to maintain a relationship with your teen that isn't always focused on the ways he disappoints you. Invite him to participate in family activities and things you might enjoy doing together; your teen is still someone you love, despite your anger, and there's always the possibility of being together in positive ways.

Natural, Real-Life Consequences

The most effective consequences, those that have the highest likelihood of teaching lessons, are those that occur naturally in the real world. They are not imposed by you. In the case of illegal activities, you might be tempted to hire legal representation so that charges can be dismissed or expunged. This might seem helpful—no parent wants their child to have "a record"—and yet it also teaches your teen that he can "get off" when others try to hold him accountable. Parents who try to protect their teens from the natural consequences of their behaviors often find that the behaviors continue.

While no parent wants their teen to spend time in jail, it may be most effective not to rescue your teen and to let him experience some of the real-life consequences to his behavior. The middle path is to help your teen face the legal system *and* encourage his lawyers to mandate community service and/or treatment rather than jail. In that case, there would be a negative consequence *and* the hope that your teen will learn enough to change some of his behaviors.

If you've tried all that you can to help your teen lessen his aggression or violence in your home, the next step might be to engage the authorities, especially if he's refusing or not responding to treatment. Although it's very painful to do so, you *can* charge your teen with assault if he's been violent toward you or any member of the family. Sometimes the best opportunity you have to get your teen the help he needs is to have treatment or structure mandated by the court.

The natural consequence for illegal, dangerous, or aggressive behavior may be the legal system as well as the loss of trust between you and your teen. Both will affect the way he can live his life until he is able to make the changes he needs to make.

Don't Threaten Unless You Can Follow Through

You may wonder, during especially difficult times, if you should tell your teen or young adult (over eighteen years old) that he can no longer live at home if he doesn't follow your rules or is aggressive. You might think this action will provide some relief from the ongoing struggle or teach him a lesson. It's also sometimes the one consequence parents have at their disposal when a teen or young adult doesn't respond to limit setting. However, it's not effective to make this threat unless you're able and willing to follow through if he doesn't change his behavior. If you're not prepared to follow through because this is a very hard thing to do, don't make the threat; it only teaches him that you don't mean what you say, which makes it harder to set any limits in the future.

Assessing Positive and Negative Consequences of Your Decisions

You'll probably only entertain the option of having your older teen live elsewhere if you're very frustrated and have already tried other options, all of which have been unsuccessful. This decision cannot be made lightly and should not be made emotionally. It's important to assess positive and negative consequences before threatening him with responses that you may not follow through with. There are potential negative or dangerous consequences that parents need to be aware of. Below you will find some of the possible positive and negative consequences of two options, letting your teen stay in your home despite illegal or disruptive behaviors or telling your teen he has to leave your home.

Continuing to Allow Your Teen to Live at Home

Positive Consequences

- He'll have a "safe haven" within your home and may be safer from outside dangers.

- You'll have some way to monitor his activities.

- You can maintain some relationship with him, especially during those times when he's more emotionally stable.

- You'll feel less guilty about yourself as a parent.

Negative Consequences

- He'll continue to be disruptive in the home, possibly without consequence, which will add to your anger and frustration.

- If you have other children, they may be emotionally affected or even put in danger by their sibling's behaviors or the consequences of those behaviors (such as police coming to your home).

- He may not have any incentive to change his behaviors.

- *You* may be open to legal issues, if illegal activities continue to occur in your home.

- You may have to continue to live in your own home in a way that's uncomfortable and disconcerting to you.

Telling Your Teen He Can No Longer Live at Home

Positive Consequences

- Your home may be calmer.

- You can unlock your doors and not worry about your valuables.

- He may learn that behaviors have real consequences.

- He may have an incentive to change his behaviors.

- Your other child(ren) will feel safer.

Negative Consequences

- You may lose any relationship with your teen and any ability to help him.

- There are not many services for a teen like this, and he may be on his own without any help or supervision.

- He may become homeless or put himself into more dangerous situations.

- You may become more worried and anxious about him and feel guilty about your decision.

- He may be hurt, victimized, or even die.

Some parents find that they have to ask their teen to leave because the home is no longer safe for them or other children. At times, this leads the teen to get the help that is needed or to make significant changes in his life. Other parents, who assess these positive and negative consequences, find that they cannot ask their teen to leave. They continue to be as effective as they can in helping him to get the help he needs, to set limits to the best of their ability, and to do whatever is needed to create safety in their home for all family members.

Only Your Teen Can Change His Behaviors

Ultimately, your teen will only change when he's willing to do the hard work of learning and implementing healthier behaviors. You can (1) provide an environment that reinforces safe and legal behaviors, (2) talk about the consequences of risky or illegal behaviors, (3) provide opportunities for the teen to get help, (4) reward skillful, legal, moral, and safe behaviors, and (5) allow natural consequences to occur. Still, only your teen can change himself, and he may or may not have the incentive, ability, or will to change in this moment. While you do all you can to keep your teen and your family safe, you can continue to hope that your teen will make the changes only he can make.

Acceptance

How can you accept the disruptive, substance-abusing, illegal, and/or risky activities of your teen? It's extremely difficult and incredibly painful to watch your teen seemingly dismiss the values you taught him or behave in ways you never could have expected. It's embarrassing, and isolating, to have the police at your home or to go to court proceedings.

Acceptance doesn't mean that you like what's going on or that you're giving up on your teen. It doesn't mean that you'll allow yourself to be verbally abused. It means that you know what's happening, you recognize and acknowledge the level of difficulties your teen has, and you relieve your own suffering by being willing to look at the reality of your life. Acceptance frees up your emotional energy to try to problem-solve so that you can help your teen in the most effective manner. And it also enables you to enjoy and appreciate any moments of peace and pleasure that you might be able to share with your teen.

You might not be able to change your teen, and he may not make significant changes in his life until well into adulthood, if at all. It may become less and less possible to maintain any kind of a relationship, and you may watch your teen drift further and further from the life you expected him to have. And yet you still love him, and you'll be available when he's ready to make the changes that he needs to make. Despite all the difficulties your teen may experience and despite how painful it is for you, you still have to live *your* life as fully as possible while you continue to hope for a better future for your teen.

Summary

You as parents can be most effective when you understand and accept the emotional difficulties that lead to disruptive or risky behaviors. You can also help your teen by making changes in how you respond to these behaviors.

Key Points:

- There are underlying emotional reasons why a teen may be aggressive, engage in risky or illegal behaviors, or abuse substances.

- It's important to maintain limits and expectations, even if the teen doesn't follow them or becomes threatening or dangerous when told about them.

- Natural consequences may be effective in helping your teen to learn and change his behaviors, and you may need to allow them to occur.

- Reward is a powerful change agent.

- You can benefit from accepting that you cannot change your teen and also continuing to do as much as you can to provide an environment in which change is possible and supported.

Chapter 7

When Anxiety Disrupts Life, School, and Independence

You will find this chapter relevant if your teen or young adult has any of the following behaviors: school avoidance, debilitating fears, failure to separate from you as parents, withdrawal from friends or activities, obsessive or compulsive behaviors, rigidity, perfectionism, anxiety-related medical problems, panic attacks.

Anxiety is a common emotional response that we all feel when we experience something as threatening or dangerous. It's an early warning signal that motivates us to avoid, escape, or fix problems. Anxiety can be all encompassing, affecting thinking, feeling, and behaviors. In teens who have intense emotions, anxiety can, in fact, take over their lives in a variety of ways.

Teens who experience intense anxiety sometimes keep their feelings hidden inside, making it difficult for anyone to know how overwhelmed they may be. You may have noticed that your teen feels "stressed" often, or may hesitate to take risks or try new things. These behaviors often result in avoiding certain activities and curtailing her life experiences. Fears about facing challenges and uncertainty, which are an inevitable part of growing up, limit the ability to progress into adulthood. Anxiety can be paralyzing and crippling. If your teen's behaviors and activities are limited by anxiety, you may worry about how withdrawn she is and that she's not enjoying the activities that her friends are. Anxious teens tend to have, or create, worried, exasperated, and often sad parents who don't know how to help them.

When anxiety is sudden and intense, it may be experienced as a panic attack, which has certain physiological responses. Your teen may have trouble breathing, feel faint, feel her heart racing, and think that the causes are medical. In response, you may worry about her physical wellness and take her to a physician to rule out medical issues that might cause similar physiological symptoms. Eventually, it may become clear that the cause of her physical symptoms, which are experienced as a panic attack, is anxiety, and your teen will need to learn healthier ways to manage her feelings to diminish the physical manifestations of the anxiety.

Anxiety symptoms may include irritability, rigidity, and outbursts. Your teen may become overfocused on gaining as much control over the world around her as she can in order to manage her feelings of anxiety. The attempts that she makes to control her environment (and you) and her difficulty being flexible in many situations may leave you feeling exasperated, frustrated, and angry. You, and others, might see her as "needing to have everything her way." The irritability, inflexibility, difficulty compromising, and even the distractibility and anger that you see in your teen mask her extreme anxiety. These symptoms, in turn, affect her ability to have a full life, which often requires flexibility and compromise.

In this chapter, we'll help you understand the impact that intense anxiety has on your teen's life and the different ways in which the very strong urge to avoid or control anxiety-provoking situations tends to limit her activities and life choices. We'll also provide practical advice and guidance if you wonder how much to (1) push your teen beyond her comfort zone, (2) protect her from situations that make her anxious, and/or (3) accept that her anxiety may not entirely disappear and your teen's life, therefore, may be different or more difficult than you had anticipated.

Understanding Anxiety-Driven Behaviors

Everyone experiences anxiety at times. It's not usually problematic, and it is often useful. For example, preparing for a test, obeying the law, or being conscientious are often the result of the worries and fears we have in situations where we wonder about how well we'll do or how we should behave. At the same time, some of the behaviors we use to lower or avoid anxiety can also create problems.

For some teens, the cause of their anxiety may be clear to others (such as a fear of heights or social situations). For other teens, it may be hard to identify a cause, and the anxiety seems to pervade the teen's very existence. Here are some less easily identified causes of anxiety for teens:

- the worry that they'll fail to meet their own, sometimes perfectionistic, expectations

- pervasive worry that something has been forgotten or not completed

- worries about losing control or that something *may* happen that they cannot control

- uncertainty and/or facing the unknown

- worries about the negative consequences of actions

The common denominator in these causes of anxiety is discomfort and fear—fear of a situation or outcome—and the desire to avoid the feelings associated with the fear. Anxiety is often the underlying factor in some of the behavioral problems you may have heard about or be witnessing, such as phobias, shyness, obsessive-compulsive behaviors, panic, and post-traumatic stress responses.

You may feel confused that you can't always tell what causes your teen's anxiety and therefore you don't understand why her behaviors are so limited. You can't see that your teen may be worrying about something that *might* happen. In order to lessen the intensity of her feelings, she may avoid situations that cause her fear or worry; her avoidance is then reinforced by the relief she feels when she gets away from the source of her anxiety. She might obsess or ruminate about multiple scenarios to manage her fears that, while providing some control in the moment, may cause more anxiety over time. In these situations, your teen's avoidance means she doesn't learn from experiencing and managing the situation, and her obsessing and ruminating means that she wastes time preparing for consequences that may not occur. Avoidance and escape, or obsessively trying to figure out how to manage a perceived threat, become the problematic behaviors that limit your teen's life.

Here's an example: A young person asks for help in the classroom and the teacher's response leaves her feeling "stupid." As a result, she becomes more hesitant to ask for help so she won't feel stupid again. She then doesn't ask for help when she needs it, stops asking questions when confused, and loses the opportunity to get the help she needs. This creates more anxiety. Her response to her anxiety actually exacerbates her anxiety! As a parent, you might find yourself encouraging your teen to ask for help, and you may become frustrated when she doesn't do so. You see so clearly that the more she avoids asking for help, the more she struggles and the less opportunity she has to learn that others can be supportive and that she won't always feel "stupid." Much to your dismay and frustration, instead of learning how to approach these situations and get the help she needs, she continues to avoid them because avoidance reduces her anxiety immediately and, thus, is reinforced.

Generalized Anxiety and Its Effect on Development

While many fears are learned from experience, you may notice that your teen has always been somewhat anxious, and no single situation seems to have caused this. This is called *generalized anxiety*, which impacts multiple areas of a teen's life. When your child was young, you may have noticed that her temperament made it difficult for her to adjust to change, transitions, or new situations. She may have been cautious when meeting new people or slow to join in with other kids in social situations. Her discomfort with new situations likely caused her to avoid these situations when possible. As a result, she had less opportunity to learn coping skills for managing this discomfort or the skills necessary to be successful in social situations. She may seek out only what makes her comfortable, and she may feel so anxious about new experiences that she gets angry at you when you encourage her to participate in activities or try new things. When she does have to experience something new, her anxiety increases because she has not learned how to effectively handle any new situation or her feelings. She continues to find ways to avoid or escape, often with anger and defiance. You, like many parents, may be surprised to learn that the angry outbursts and irritability that you experience with your teen are often caused by underlying anxiety.

Anxiety-Driven Behaviors

You, like other parents, may find it difficult to recognize behaviors as anxiety driven. Your teen might be embarrassed about her anxiety and pretend that everything's okay, avoid discussions of the behavior, try to convince you that her behavior makes sense, or not tell you the truth about (and sometimes not even be aware of) situations she has avoided. It's understandable that you might get angry or frustrated by these behaviors. However, when you recognize and acknowledge that the behaviors you see as rejecting your limits and expectations and perceive as defiant are actually responses to anxiety, you'll be more understanding and respond more effectively.

School Issues

Some teens are so overwhelmed and paralyzed by their anxiety about school-related issues that they don't attend school. Schools provide many opportunities for fears and worries, and a teen who has intense and overwhelming anxiety may find many reasons not to attend. Young people may avoid situations in which they worry about (1) fitting in or being rejected by peers, (2) not being able to perform up to their own, very high expectations, (3) disappointing teachers, parents, or themselves, and/or (4) being separated from, or abandoned by, parents or friends. Students may be so stressed by their own fears of failure that they don't complete schoolwork, despite how capable they appear to others. This self-perpetuating and self-fulfilling cycle may seem familiar to you: your teen feels overwhelmed by schoolwork or self-imposed social expectations and then doesn't do what she needs to do, which results in her not being able to go to school because she feels so far behind. The initial relief felt by avoiding school leads, paradoxically, to ever more anxiety and poorer school functioning.

Some teens approach school in an all-or-nothing manner, expecting perfection from themselves. Some of these students ultimately avoid handing in assignments that do not measure up to their unrealistic expectations, resulting in poor grades, shame, and sometimes even depression. Others expend so much energy trying to produce an A+ product that they cry, despair, and melt down, losing valuable work time and becoming even more emotional as a result. Despite its great emotional cost, these students may ultimately achieve at very high levels, which reinforces their ongoing struggle for perfection.

Despite their protests to the contrary, young people know that school is where they belong, and most teens actively participate in the school day despite its stresses and issues. A teen who is overwhelmed by anxiety and not able to go to school may be embarrassed and ashamed by her inability to do what most of her peers seem to have no problem doing. In addition to her shame, she may develop feelings of anger and hopelessness.

Anxiety can also cause physical symptoms (such as stomach and gut issues, headaches, back and neck pain), and some teens don't want to go to school because they feel physically ill. Because the physical discomfort provides an excuse not to go to school, and may even draw sympathy and caring from others, it may be reinforced and continue. The physical illness and pain are real, do make it difficult to attend school, *and* may be related to and exacerbated by the anxiety.

It's understandably hard to return after an absence or after a perceived failure, and the longer a student stays out of school, the harder it is to come back. Her fears and anxieties continue to escalate, and she doesn't experience opportunities that might prove successful and lessen her fears. If, for example, she were able to attend school, she might realize that she can do the work, speak to her peers, and generally handle what she needs to do. As long as she's out of school, she experiences fewer and fewer opportunities to learn how to manage her anxieties in an effective manner. While she may be comfortable staying home, she's most likely struggling to find ways to manage the pain and suffering that paralyzes her so that she can have the life she wants to have.

Teens who approach school with a perfectionistic attitude often have the belief that high school performance predicts adult success. In fact, high school performance does *not* predict adult success. These students work hard and may achieve at high levels, while their anxiety negatively affects other areas of their lives and development as they reach adulthood.

School issues don't always translate into social concerns. Teens who may have difficulty attending school or who may be too ill to attend school may still remain connected to friends through social media during the day and at activities after school. While these social connections may be healthy for your teen, you will feel conflicted by what you see as a contradiction in her behavior. We will discuss how to resolve this issue later in this chapter when we discuss exposure and strategically using reinforcers and negative consequences.

Rigid and Obsessive-Compulsive Behaviors

Some teens respond to their anxiety about uncertainty by trying to control as much of their environment as they can. You may notice that your teen insists on doing things in a certain way, may become angry and possibly even aggressive if there is deviation from the way she thinks she needs it to be, or may take a very long time to complete certain tasks (such as homework, personal hygiene, even leaving the house). These behaviors continue to narrow the life of your teen and lead to increased worry for you. You may often find yourself inadvertently supporting your teen's anxiety-driven behaviors (by checking things for her or helping her to complete tasks) in order to "move things along" or avoid outbursts. This response reinforces your teen's behaviors and doesn't provide opportunities for her to learn healthier ways to manage her anxiety.

Teens who engage in rituals or rigid, compulsive behaviors (hand washing, making lists, counting, checking over and over to make sure things are done perfectly) are usually aware that they're behaving differently. They may be embarrassed or ashamed by these behaviors and might not trust anyone (even treatment providers or best friends) enough to tell them about their fears, thoughts, or rituals. Teens who manage their anxiety in this way may go out of their way to hide their behaviors, engaging in them secretly. They may respond with anger or frustration, sometimes aggressively, if they are "found out" or prevented from engaging in the behavior that they feel the need to do, and without which they feel totally out of control and an overwhelming sense of anxiety.

Validation and acceptance are necessary to set the stage for your teen to do the very hard work of exposing herself to an uncertain world without the comfort of the behaviors she has relied on. Like a child giving up her blanket, your teen will eventually need to let go of the behaviors she feels have kept her safe and develop new skills in order to live a life of satisfaction.

Failure to Move into Adulthood

Some teens and young adults who experience anxiety may have difficulty taking independent steps toward adulthood. Older teens who may have been able to cover their fear of the unknown in the structured environments of home and school often experience tremendous anxiety. Their fear may surface, or be exacerbated, when the next steps that they face in life are more uncertain and may occur in an unfamiliar environment.

If your teen feels that she isn't capable of, or is too anxious to, manage new or independent activities—such as academic work or a job—and worries about failing or otherwise embarrassing herself, she may remain stuck at home. Or your older teen may ultimately leave home only to have her anxiety and lack of skills get in the way of effectively and safely managing her independence. She may then return home and be unable or unwilling to take further steps forward.

Your older adolescent may appear unmotivated or unwilling to do anything productive, like take a college or trade-related course or get a job, and you may be distressed by what you see as her lack of activity or direction. It may seem to you that she's lazy and "likes" being taken care of. You may become judgmental if she remains socially active while not taking on any adult responsibilities. When you remember that she may actually be doing the best she can in this moment and may, in fact, be constrained by her anxiety and fears, you'll be less emotionally reactive and more validating, even while you continue to encourage more adult-like behaviors.

When teens are unable to move on to the activities that their peers are engaging in, or fail at their attempts to keep up with others, they recognize that they want to have a fuller life, and yet they are unable to muster the skills to face their anxieties about the unknown future. While they may appear "unmotivated" or "lazy," they are really quite anxious and feel unprepared to move forward. Your older teen may resist your well-meaning encouragement or pressure to improve her life by engaging in meaningful activities, or she may make numerous attempts and find herself unable to complete or be successful at any of them. In either scenario, she begins to fear any new attempts and avoids them in order to minimize the anxiety she feels.

Your teen may deny anxieties, hide behind anger and irritability, or minimize anxiety-provoking interactions by spending a great deal of time withdrawing and doing little except sleeping or spending time on her computer. You may witness her retreating from activities with friends who have moved on with their lives, and you may despair that she will ever catch up. She may actually be quite distressed about her life and may also become depressed. The longer this behavior continues, the harder it is for her to recognize that she can make significant changes in her life. While your young adult who is "stuck" may get angry if you encourage her to try new activities, she may very well need that encouragement—given in a validating, gentle way—in order to experience success and find a way to have a life that is worthwhile and meaningful for her.

Parental Responses to Anxiety-Driven Behaviors

Anxiety-driven behaviors may worry and confuse you, as they do other parents, especially when your teen's anxiety is covered up or expressed as defiance, anger, or a physical ailment. You may feel reluctant to "push" your teen when she seems ill, and you may inadvertently reinforce the symptoms with extra attention or privileges; or, alternatively, you may demand compliance and engage in an unwinnable power struggle when she will not comply with your requests or expectations. Even when you understand that anxiety is at the root of the problem, you may not know how to respond. Here are some questions that parents like you ask when their teen has anxiety-driven behaviors:

- "How much do I protect my teen from sources of anxiety, and how much do I encourage her to face them?"

- "How much do I lessen my expectations of my teen to make her less stressed?"

- "Do I let my teen participate in activities she enjoys on days when she doesn't comply with expectations?"

- "How do I help my teen without overwhelming her?"

- "How do I respond to rigidity and unwillingness to compromise without getting angry?"

We will respond to these questions through a discussion of the following vignette:

> Magda, a high school sophomore, had always been shy, and it was often hard for her to try new activities or meet new people. She contracted an infection during the school year and missed almost three consecutive weeks of school. As she recovered, she began to express anxiety about returning to school and said she was worried about people asking her a lot of questions about why she was out. On the day she was to return, she wouldn't go. She asked for one more day to get prepared. The day turned into several, and she has now been out of school an additional two weeks. She becomes angry and verbally threatens her parents when they encourage her to go to school. She has avoided communicating with her friends and spends the day interacting with new friends she has made online. Her parents don't know what to do. Whenever they broach the subject of returning to

school, Magda gets upset and says she'll do it tomorrow, yet the pattern repeats. Additionally, she has begun calling her parents when they're at work to make sure they're safe. Although she had always asked for a lot of reassurance, this feels overwhelming to her parents and they don't know how to respond.

Validation

When you are confronted by your teen's anxiety-driven behaviors, you might respond in a number of ways. Some parents may be tempted to do things like these:

- provide support in the form of reassurance, which inadvertently invalidates their teen's experience by minimizing it ("You and I both know you can do this work.")

- dismiss the anxiety altogether in order to encourage the teen to participate in activities that make her anxious ("There's nothing to be worried about. Let's just go.")

- protect the teen from any anxiety by allowing her to avoid situations where she experiences anxiety ("I know you don't feel well. You don't have to go to school today.")

You may be confused about how to provide support and reassurance in ways that both acknowledge the underlying feelings and that do not justify, or reinforce, the behavior. You may find yourself inadvertently minimizing your teen's anxiety when you are trying to provide support ("Things will be okay..."). Or you may inadvertently enable behaviors that you would really like to decrease. When your teen has anxiety, it is very important to be mindful of your responses so that you can effectively validate the emotions and not the behaviors.

Acknowledge Your Own Feelings

If your teen increasingly withdraws and is unwilling to attend school or other activities, becomes more rigid in her routines, or seems so overwhelmed that she appears paralyzed, you will understandably be both scared and frustrated. If she will do some activities and not others, you may become confused and angry as well. And when your teen seems to need constant support from you, it might become overwhelming, as it did for Magda's parents in the vignette. Magda's parents might also have thoughts and feelings like these:

- embarrassment that their daughter is not attending school

- feeling incompetent as parents since they're not able to do something so "basic" as getting their daughter to school

- feeling blame (actual or perceived) from others for not being able to get their daughter to school

- conflicted about wanting to help their daughter feel better while also getting her to school

- confusion about how to provide support and reassurance for their daughter while also managing their own lives and responsibilities

- anger over her demands for their time and guilt about that anger because they recognize that she has problems

When your teen is anxious, it's easy to understand why you feel anxious as well. The opposite is also true; your anxiety may increase your teen's anxiety. Anxiety, like most emotions, is contagious, and within a family one person's anxiety can increase another's. While your teen worries about social and school issues, you worry about her, how to make her life easier, and how to help her cope with life. You may become worried that her inability to manage anxiety in a healthy way will negatively affect her future.

When your teen's rigid, controlling, or perfectionistic behaviors and poor management of tasks or activities begin to affect your family life, your own anxiety may become anger and frustration. It may be hard for you not to give in to your teen's demands because you're worried about her reaction. You'll find it helpful to balance your needs, the needs of your whole family, and the needs of your teen so that she doesn't negatively affect other family members. You'll learn to validate the feelings of your teen while still expecting her to meet her responsibilities and to adapt, when necessary, to the needs of the family and of the outside world.

Acknowledge What's Real to Your Teen

Anxiety is real. It may be hidden and it may not make rational sense. Still, it is felt emotionally and physically and it can be paralyzing. Think about a time that you felt anxious or uncomfortable, even if as a child. Your fears may not have been rational *and* they still felt real. This is what your teen feels, an overwhelming dread of *something*. She may be embarrassed and ashamed by her fears and thus suffer even more. You can help your teen by acknowledging the anxiety and what she might be afraid of.

In Magda's case, Magda's parents might acknowledge that Magda (1) is uncomfortable about having missed so much school, (2) worries about her schoolwork and how her peers or teachers will respond to her when she returns, (3) feels like an outsider since she has been away for so long, (4) feels more comfortable and less anxious at home than she would feel at school, and (5) still experiences anxiety, even at home.

The challenge you and parents like Magda's face in a situation like this is to validate your teen's feelings without providing false assurance or agreeing with her behaviors. Here are some of the statements that Magda's parents might make:

- "It makes sense that it would be hard to go back to school after being away for so long. It's hard for anyone to return after an absence."

- "Of course it feels more comfortable to stay home and it feels strange to go back to school."

- "It's understandable that you're worried about your schoolwork."

- "We know that you're worried about us. Is there any way that we can help you feel better about this?"

When you're frustrated that your teen is rigid and attempting to control many aspects of family life, recognize that she is driven by certain needs and fears that may appear inexplicable to you and are all important to her. Validate her feelings by noting how difficult it is to face the unknown and uncertainty and how hard it must be to feel so out of control at times. When you acknowledge the anxiety that your teen experiences, *you* are able to be less anxious, angry, and less emotionally reactive; this will enable you to be more validating of her feelings. While you may still feel frustrated and confused, lessening the intensity of your emotions makes it easier to think wisely, solve problems, and arrive at the most effective way to both validate and help your teen move forward.

Reducing Anxiety: Experiencing What's Feared

Your impulse as a parent is to protect your teen who's anxious in those situations that cause her the most distress. She may request relief from pressures or activities that cause her to feel physically ill or emotionally stressed, and it makes sense that you would want to provide this relief. And yet, without the opportunity to successfully experience the feared activity, she won't learn how to tolerate, manage, and lessen her anxiety and lead a fuller life. Your role, then, is to encourage her to experience what she fears while also providing comfort, support, and soothing activities to help her manage her anxiety during the experience.

The way that people learn to manage anxiety and stop avoiding feared activities is through experiencing them in manageable doses so they can develop the skills and ability to cope with their fears. (In clinical settings, this is referred to as *exposure*.) Often, teens who have anxiety-driven behaviors will work with a mental health professional to develop and implement a behavior plan that enables them to increase their ability to manage situations that usually cause anxiety. They are taught to experience what makes them anxious while also being taught and encouraged to use soothing techniques and not being allowed to avoid what they fear or use behaviors that distract themselves or others from what is expected. The teen learns to manage, rather than avoid, those situations effectively and skillfully.

As difficult as it is, you'll be most effective when you prevent your teen from avoiding or controlling all anxiety-producing activities and when you gently, and with much understanding and validation, ask your teen to face what she fears. It's through these challenges that coping skills grow and develop and your teen can begin to experience her life to the fullest.

Magda's parents will both validate her feelings and encourage her to experience being in school. At first, she may only go to the school and sit in the parking lot, or meet with the guidance counselor, or walk in the door in order to be exposed to the school building. Her parents will provide support, validation, and comfort. They won't provide an escape from the situation by taking her home before she has entered the building. This, as any parent can imagine, may take some time and may be very stressful for both Magda and her parents. After a few days of entering the building, Magda may be expected to attend a class or two. She will be told in advance that she will not be expected to participate or answer questions unless she feels comfortable doing so. After Magda begins attending class, she may add another class, or be expected to ask one question or speak to one person. In this way, she's being exposed to attending class and interacting with people in school, two of the issues that have kept her from school. Magda will gradually increase her time in school, knowing that she can speak to the guidance counselor if she feels anxious and that she will *not* be allowed to leave school earlier than the predetermined time.

If your teen has ritualized or controlling behaviors—such as excessive hand washing, constantly asking for reassurance, or unnecessary and repetitive checking for danger—you'll also need to work hard at not inadvertently supporting these behaviors. While life may feel more peaceful and easier if you simply give in to your teen, this will allow these behaviors to continue, and your teen will not make necessary and healthy changes. She will learn to be more flexible when she is gently, and with validation, encouraged to use healthier coping skills instead of her controlling behaviors.

Exposure and Strategically Using Reinforcement/ Reward and Punishment/Negative Consequences

Magda's parents are fully aware of her struggle to attend school. They may be tempted to make her life easier and less stressful by allowing her privileges during the time that she isn't in school, or when she hasn't completed the tasks associated with becoming less anxious by doing what is expected of her (facing her fears) so that she can overcome her anxiety. If they do this, it won't be effective because it provides little incentive for Magda to do the hard work of the exposure (facing and experiencing what she fears) required to return to school and get better. When Magda doesn't meet expectations (by going to school), her parents will be most effective in fostering long-term change by limiting her access to computers and other activities; they can use those activities as reinforcers (rewards) when she completes her tasks and/or goes to school. Like many parents, Magda's parents may worry that this is punitive because Magda cannot help her anxiety. But this consequence isn't punitive; it is, instead, a motivation for Magda to change her behaviors, and it needs to be accepted as such. Magda can continue to receive validation for her feelings, even as the expectations of her behaviors continue to evolve.

If your teen has controlling, rigid, or perfectionistic behaviors, it's also important to allow her to experience her anxiety when she isn't able to control situations. For example, if your teen has to hand in a paper on a certain date and is going over and over it, it would not be helpful for you to write an excuse so that she does not have to hand in the paper on time. It is more effective to let her hand in a paper that she may feel is less than perfect and learn to manage her anxiety about that. The exposure in these situations is to face uncertainty, to not have what she feels she needs, and to not be in control. It's only when your teen is able to experience her anxiety, rather than avoid it, that she will learn that she can ultimately manage it effectively.

Balanced Parenting: When to Push and When to Protect

The question that parents ask most often is when to push their teen to face her fears and when to protect her from what she fears. You may wonder how you'll know where and when to draw the line. How do you know when you're expecting too little or when you're expecting too much? It makes sense that you want to protect your teen as much as possible from the things that cause her stress. At the same time, when you expect little or protect too much, your teen may not push herself to try to do more or ever step outside her comfort zone. Your teen may paradoxically feel less capable and more fragile, and will believe even more that she isn't able to manage her anxiety. Your fears can exacerbate hers. Your teen benefits most when she knows you believe in her abilities even when *she* doesn't. She'll "borrow" your confidence, belief, and hope until she's able to generate them herself. It's important, therefore, as you validate your teen, that you also express your own belief that she can manage even when she doesn't think this herself and even if she seems overwhelmed by what you ask of her.

At the same time, if you set your expectations too high, you will experience even more resistance from your teen, who may shut down entirely and believe she's totally incapable. The resolution is to find a balance between pushing her to do *a little* more than she thinks she can do (go to the school building, talk to a teacher or a peer for a minute, approach a feared object just until it's within sight) and *not* demanding too much of her or asking her to move faster than she actually can (go to school for the whole day or touch a feared object). You can see the potential positive and negative consequences of pushing or protecting below:

Pushing Your Teen

Positive Consequences

- She'll learn that she can handle certain situations.

- She'll feel the confidence you have in her.

- She won't feel fragile.

- She'll feel empowered.

Negative Consequences

- You and she will be more anxious.

- She may be more angry.

- She may "dig in" and refuse to do even more.

- She may continue to feel like she's failing or disappointing others.

Protecting Your Teen

Positive Consequences

- You and she will be calmer in the short run.

- There will be less anger and frustration between you.

- She may be grateful that you understand her, and protecting her from what she fears may enhance your relationship.

Negative Consequences

- She'll continue to feel that she can't handle situations.

- She'll feel more fragile and less capable.

- She may not learn how to manage her feelings, how to face uncertainty, or how to live independently.

- She won't be able to take risks or learn new behaviors.

You can effectively parent your teen who is anxious by (1) recognizing her strengths *and* limitations, and taking both into consideration when establishing expectations, (2) pushing a little while also protecting a little, (3) gradually increasing what you expect of her, *while* (4) validating her anxiety and fears. You'll be most effective if you are constantly aware of and communicating a balance of acceptance (acknowledging that your adolescent experiences anxiety that is real and difficult for her) and change (encouraging more effective responses to anxiety).

Acceptance

Teens and young adults who feel anxiety often feel emotionally isolated and alone. The embarrassment that may result from their anxiety-driven behaviors can be challenging for them to manage. Your teen needs to know that, even though her emotions might be more intense than others, anxiety is a part of life that *she can, and will, learn to manage* so that she can live the life she wants. While she learns to manage her anxiety and fears, she needs the understanding and acceptance of those around her.

As a parent, it may be difficult to accept that your teen struggles in her daily life and that life is more difficult for her than it might be for others. You might be tempted to minimize her anxiety or dismiss it. Or you might worry that if you accept it, you are resigned to your teen's ongoing struggles and to giving up hope for change. Acceptance doesn't mean giving up hope; it means acknowledging the very real feelings that your teen experiences. Your teen needs acceptance so that she can face her struggles and the very difficult task of changing her behavior. If she is going to stop avoiding and start experiencing, you'll need to be her cheerleader, acknowledging how difficult it is to try new things or face certain fears and also believing in her and hoping with her for an end to her struggles. You and your teen may feel better when you accept that the journey to adulthood may be walked in a variety of different ways. Your acceptance will let her know that she can take this journey in her own way while she takes the steps she needs to achieve her goals and live the life she wants to lead.

Summary

If your teen has anxiety-driven behaviors, this most often will mean that she will avoid or escape from situations she fears. You can help her by balancing your acknowledgment of her anxiety with your expectation that she do what she fears.

Key Points:

- Anxiety is a typical physiological response that, when intense, may result in your teen avoiding difficult or painful situations or becoming overfocused on certain situations.

- Your teen learns that she can manage stressful situations by being exposed to them.

- When your teen has controlling or rigid behaviors, you will be most effective if you don't inadvertently reinforce these behaviors by supporting them.

- As a parent, you are most effective when you find the balance between pushing your teen to try harder *and* protecting her a little so that she's not overwhelmed by anxiety.

- Wise parenting means balancing acceptance and change—validating the anxiety and asking your teen to do a little more.

Chapter 8

Disordered Eating Behaviors

This chapter is for you if your teen or young adult has any of the following behaviors: restricting or not eating, bingeing (eating great amounts of food at one time), vomiting after eating, excessive focus on body weight or shape.

For some teens, eating becomes a problem as they physically develop and become more conscious of their appearance and weight. Eating may even become, much to your dismay and consternation as parents, the focus of their lives and the dominating theme in their behaviors. These teens may restrict their calorie intake or eat large quantities of food. Some teens may take laxatives or force themselves to vomit as a way to purge the food from their bodies and, they think, to maintain their weight. While disordered eating behaviors are most commonly associated with females, they occur in males as well.

Many teens were "picky eaters" growing up. They may not have liked many foods as a child, and mealtimes may have been a struggle. Some of these children grow up and still only like a limited number of foods while remaining healthy. Others experiment by becoming vegetarians and vegans and may maintain these behaviors into adulthood. Most become more flexible with eating as they get older and grow into healthy-eating teens and adults. Some teens may have had no eating issues growing up and may develop a focus on food as they get older.

Whether your teen was a "picky eater" or had no issues around food, she may develop more restricted or poorly controlled eating habits over time as she uses food as a way to manage her emotions and exercise control over her life. And she may do all of this in private due to shame and embarrassment. As a parent, your teen's unhealthy eating behaviors are a major concern, and you, like other parents, understandably worry about ongoing heath issues related to eating too little or eating too much.

An Important Notice

If your teen has symptoms consistent with anorexia, characterized by low body weight and restricting calories, it is important that you seek the specialized treatment for this condition. Anorexia can result in death and treatment is crucial.

This chapter will help those of you whose teens or young adults have disordered eating characterized by a combination of restricting, bingeing, and purging. You may watch as your teen severely restricts her diet or seems to eat nothing at all or, at the other extreme, eats whatever food is available and then disappears after meals to throw it up. If you're facing any of these issues related to disordered eating, we'll help you find answers to your questions about whether to push your teen to eat or eat less, or leave her alone so as not to "make food an issue." We will also help you manage your own anxiety and respond to questions about the health of your teen.

Understanding Disordered Eating Behaviors

Disordered eating is another way that your teen may attempt to manage emotional pain, a sense of emptiness, or internal turmoil that is not apparent to you or others. Some teens who have disordered eating behaviors may appear quite confident, be successful academically and/or athletically, participate in activities, and/or have many friends. If this is the case with your teen, you may find it hard to appreciate or understand her feelings about herself. These might include feeling (1) not good enough, (2) out of control despite outward appearances to the contrary, (3) empty or confused inside, (4) ugly or not liking how she looks, and/or (5) unhappy or sad about her life or herself. That your teen appears so competent often masks the fragility that is just beneath the surface. And it comes as a surprise when the confident teen that you thought you knew begins to outwardly express the wide array of feelings that she is actually experiencing. While your teen may seem so successful to others in so many ways, she's really not yet competent in managing emotions. The intensity of the emotions and the inability to manage them effectively sometimes lead her to eat in ways that are not healthy in the long run.

Your teen, like many teens and young adults who have disordered eating behaviors, may also have perceptions of herself and her body that others might not share. She may (1) see or experience herself as fat when the doctor determines she's at a healthy weight, (2) want to look like the models she sees in magazines or on TV when this might not be realistic for her body shape and size, and/or (3) force herself to live up to ideal standards without being able to recognize the unrealistic or unreasonable expectations that this places on her and without accepting the negative impact on her health. Poor eating often impacts cognitive ability, so she becomes increasingly unable to see or accept the reality of her situation.

Restricting Food and Burning Calories

As your teen becomes overwhelmed by the intensity of her emotions, she may begin to count the calories in her food, restrict her food intake, and develop rigid rules about eating that begin to take over more and more of her life, masking the chaos she feels internally with a controlled veneer. She is reassuring herself that she can be in control of her life by being in control of what she eats. And yet the more she feels overwhelmed by her emotions, the more she will restrict her eating as a way to manage her emotions, which paradoxically results in developing behaviors that are increasingly out of control. The cycle continues as she seeks more control while losing the ability to recognize how out of control her life is becoming.

Restricting behavior often begins in secret as your teen wants to be in control of the situation and doesn't want feedback from others. She may lie to or deceive you as a way to continue to be in control, because she feels her life spinning out of control. If you or others make any attempt to encourage her to eat in a healthier way, she may respond with irritability or anger. Power struggles around food become pervasive, and food becomes an ongoing source of conflict within your family.

If your teen's goal is to limit food intake, she may create "games" for herself as she pushes herself to eat less and restrict more. She may want to find out just how few calories she can exist on. She dismisses or denies that this game is a deadly one. When restricting is related to body image distortions and a desire to be thin, your teen may begin to exercise more and more. While exercise in general is a healthy activity, in teens and young adults who wish to be thinner, the exercise sometimes becomes excessive, taking over their lives and pushing them beyond the limits of what is healthy.

Because severe restricting behavior can lead to significant health issues and can be deadly, these symptoms require continual monitoring by a heath professional who is knowledgeable about disordered eating. Teens frequently load up on liquids, carry weights in their pockets, or otherwise interfere with accurate weight checks as a way to appear healthier than they might be and to interfere with proper medical assessment and care.

Bingeing and Purging

If your teen binges and purges, eating excessive amounts of often unhealthy food and then vomiting, she is trying to regulate painful and overwhelming emotions as well as fill the emptiness she feels. Unlike the teen who restricts and is comforted by *not* eating, she is actually soothed by the pleasure of eating and tries to find ways to access food. The more she engages in this behavior, the more shame and guilt she feels. She then struggles to manage these overwhelming emotions, which results in eating more, and the cycle continues.

Your teen who binges may also be concerned about her weight, and since she cannot keep herself from eating huge quantities of food, she will look for ways to rid herself of the food and the calories, either through the use of laxatives or by inducing vomiting under the mistaken belief that she will not gain weight. This cycle often results in gaining weight, which increases her shame and disgust with herself and further distresses her.

Bingeing and purging are usually done in secret, and teens who feel tremendous shame about the behavior will often deny it if confronted. You may become aware that food is missing or find hidden snacks (or the wrappers from the food) in bedrooms, backpacks, or other places. You may notice that your teen goes directly to the bathroom after meals. Keeping food available for other family members may become a problem and may generate even more anger and shame for the teen, who seems genuinely unable to control her eating behavior. The more emotional intensity your teen feels, the more she'll be drawn to the behavior of eating that helps her to regulate her emotions, which feel increasingly out of control.

If your teen binges and purges, she may also be very focused on body image, body shape, or weight, and may exercise excessively as a way to manage her emotions and her weight. Food and exercise may become the twin obsessions that take over her life. As a result, she may shy away from friends and activities in order to keep her behaviors secret from others.

At first, she feels good about her behaviors and begins to feel more in control of her life and emotions. She will usually resist attempts to label the behavior a problem and will explain her behaviors to others as "just watching my weight" and "caring about how I look." She may actually see her behaviors as healthy. As the bingeing and purging continue, however, and begin to take over her life, becoming the focus of most of her thinking and many of her behaviors, she may feel more shame and, ultimately, less in control.

At some point, she may realize that her behaviors cannot be explained or excused, and yet she may feel powerless to make any changes. Her shame becomes anger and even belligerence if she is confronted or asked to change or modify her behaviors. She's caught in the dilemma of either feeling good and managing her mood at the expense of her health, or maintaining her health at the expense of feeling good and managing her mood. Your teen is struggling and needs help to get better. Yet for her, the work of getting healthier feels arduous and unnecessary. She will have to find some reason why the benefits of eating in a healthier way outweigh the benefits of behaviors that help her to manage her feelings. The resolution of this dilemma and the understanding that she can actually have the life she wants if she behaves in a healthier way will contribute to her willingness to do the work of getting well.

Parental Responses to Disordered Eating Behaviors

Teens who have disordered eating—whether this means they are restricting, developing rigid rules about eating, or bingeing and purging—create great tension for their parents and within their families. As you try to fulfill what you feel is your responsibility to your teen's health by encouraging her to eat in a nutritionally sound way, you may be met with irritability and anger. Home life may involve ongoing power struggles as you encourage your teen to eat, or, alternatively, food disappears so that other family members cannot eat when they want to. You may vacillate between anger and frustration with your teen and your very understandable fears for her health.

You, like other parents, often wonder about your role in helping your teen who has disordered eating. You want to know how much you should force your teen to eat, whether or not you should lock up food in your home because your teen binges, how much to punish, and what to reinforce. You worry about how much control your teen has or doesn't have, and what impact you can have over what seem to be intractable behaviors. We will discuss these issues by looking at the vignette below:

> Diane became actively involved with sports in middle school, and in
> high school, she began focusing on fitness very seriously. Her parents

were pleased with how responsibly she took physical exercise and nutrition. In eleventh grade, she was diagnosed with a stress fracture in her foot from running, and despite warnings from her medical team that she take some time off from running and other exercise until it healed, she continued to exercise. Her parents worried that she could potentially cause more damage to her foot. They also began to notice that she would not eat for periods of time, followed by days when she ate unhealthy foods without regard for her health or wellness. They were horrified to discover through one of Diane's friends that she had been throwing up in the bathroom after eating large quantities of food. Now Diane's parents fear for her physical and mental health. When they try to talk with her about their concerns, she denies the behavior, becomes angry and verbally abusive, and tells them she's got it under control and there's no problem or cause for worry.

Validation

You may be so frustrated by your teen's unhealthy eating and so anxious about her long-term health that you cannot consider what she might be feeling or experiencing. You may become so invested in making sure she eats in healthy ways and so exhausted (or angered) by the struggle that you don't have the energy to consider your own or your teen's emotions.

If you admonish your teen to "just" eat something, you are inadvertently invalidating how hard it is for her to do what may be easy for so many others. Your understandable fears may cause her to try to exercise more control, leading to more power struggles while she feels less understood in these circumstances.

Your emotions make it much harder to be validating of your teen—which will be necessary if she is going to make any of the very difficult changes that will lead to healthier eating behaviors. Keep in mind that validating her feelings does not mean that you like her behaviors or that you will not continue to ask for a change in those behaviors.

Acknowledge Your Own Feelings

When you witness your teen's struggles around food, you may become quite anxious and concerned about her health and welfare. You may have sought help from nutritionists or medical doctors, and you may be quite frustrated when the directions and advice given your teen is ignored or dismissed. This frustration and anxiety can become anger as you and your teen struggle with each other:

Parent: "You have to eat something; remember what the doctor said."

Teen: "Leave me alone; you can't make me eat, and I don't care what the doctor says."

Every meal becomes a battle. If your teen binges, you may be very angry that food disappears and other members of the family can't have the foods they want to eat. It may be even more frustrating when you have to lock up the food in your house. The impact of these behaviors affects the whole family.

Given a situation like this with your teen, you, like most parents, will experience a mix of emotions. In the vignette, it makes sense that Diane's parents feel like this:

- frustrated and angry that she's not following doctor's advice and that she might reinjure herself

- helpless and inadequate that they cannot get their daughter to behave in a safer, healthier way

- worried that her eating behaviors will create medical issues and longer-term health problems

- embarrassed that she's vomiting and guilty that they weren't aware of this behavior

- angry that she denies the problems that they can clearly see

- helpless because they cannot discuss these issues with her without an emotional outburst

- bewildered and confused about what happened to the responsible teen they thought they were raising

- desperate to find the proper help for their daughter and despairing about how to get her to follow through on the medical advice she is given

- ashamed of their own parenting and worried that they somehow caused this behavior

- powerless that they cannot seem to fix the problem with the solutions that seem so clear to them

- anxious that their daughter might die from her disordered eating

It's important to acknowledge your very understandable emotions so that they don't cloud your ability to validate your child. At the same time, you need to accept that you cannot control your teen's behaviors, only your responses to them.

Acknowledge What's Real to Your Teen

Not easily visible behind your teen's focus on food, exercise, and/or body image is an overwhelming internal sense of chaos and emptiness. Her sense of emotionally being out of control and not knowing how to feel better is masked by her problems with food. The teen who seems so capable and competent to others feels incompetent to herself, especially in terms of how to manage her feelings. Underneath the veneer of being able to manage her life may be a teen who's scared and vulnerable. Behind the bravado may be guilt and shame.

Diane's parents will benefit from understanding that teens have certain expectations of themselves and their abilities. It's hard for these teens to accept when they aren't able to do things that have come easily in the past and helped to define their identity. Teens like Diane who are focused on the moment may not be able to delay activities that they feel they need to do now so that they might be healthier in the future. They worry that they might never be able to return to their normal activities.

Given these realities, Diane's parents might be able to acknowledge that she's feeling (1) ambivalent about the way her body looks, (2) frustrated that she can't exercise in the way she wants to, (3) scared and frustrated by the way she's managing food, (4) emotions that are confusing and over-whelming, (5) a need for some control over her life, which feels increasingly scary or out of control to her, (6) worried about her physical health and her weight, and (7) fearful and anxious about when, if ever, she'll be better and able to return to healthy eating patterns and exercise and to regain her identity as a competent and successful athlete.

You may feel the urge to reassure your teen by dismissing or minimizing her fears and anxieties by saying things like "Of course you'll be better soon. Just rest your foot as the doctor suggested and soon enough you'll be fine" or "You don't have to exercise every day—you look fine the way you are" or "You'll feel healthier if you just stop eating all that junk food." Anytime you use the word "just," you minimize the effort it takes for your teen to accept herself or her situation and to change her behaviors.

It may be difficult to find ways to validate your teen's feelings without reinforcing or supporting her unhealthy behaviors. Diane's parents, for example, might be able to validate her feelings in these ways:

- "We know that you're concerned that you'll gain weight, especially with how much emphasis our culture places on thinness."

- "It has to be really hard for you to not be able to exercise the way you want to. It's frustrating to us when we can't do the things we want to do."

- "You must be really upset about this situation, and it's hard to figure out how to manage all these feelings."

- "You must feel like you can't control what's happening in your life right now. That's got to be really hard for you."

Diane's parents cannot fix her foot and may not be able to change her eating habits. By validating her, they acknowledge what she's going through so that she doesn't feel isolated and so she feels more accepted by others. While you might be frustrated, angry, and worried about your teen's behaviors, you may be able to take yourself out of power struggles by understanding her feelings and concerns. In this way, you can focus on more effective strategies to help your teen change. Beginning a dialogue with your teen may help both of you move forward. It may also enable her to accept her situation and move toward finding healthier ways to manage her emotions.

It Takes a Team

If you're worried about your teen's eating habits and her health, it's critical that you and your teen obtain professional support to both assess her medical situation and provide guidance, directly to her, about what she needs to do to remain healthy. Often this support includes a medical doctor, a nutritionist, and a mental health practitioner. If your teen is able to develop a positive and trusting relationship with these professionals, she will be more likely, although not necessarily always willing, to follow their advice and feedback.

A medical evaluation is an important first step when you have concerns about your teen's eating and health. A doctor who is aware of the consequences of disordered eating behaviors will know what to look for and how to advise you about what to do next. As long as the doctor feels that your teen is within normal limits on her weight and blood work, you can work on lessening your anxiety and the struggles you may be having with her. When a doctor begins to express concerns, he or she should discuss them directly with the teen. It's most effective when feedback comes from others and not from you, since your teen can accuse you of "worrying too much."

Some teens respond well to working with and getting feedback from nutritionists who can provide guidance on what they need to eat and how to develop healthy eating habits. Nutritionists are effective in explaining to teens how avoiding of food and throwing up or using laxatives really create further health problems and affect the way their bodies metabolize food, which leads to more calories being stored in the body. Developing a healthy eating plan is more effective for maintaining a particular weight than is dieting, fasting, or purging. At the same time, teens often resent one more person telling them what to do and may reject any advice given to them, much to the frustration of their parents. It's important, therefore, for you to find adults in your teen's life that she trusts (like a coach, teacher, or relative) who may be able to help her change her behaviors.

If disordered eating interferes with the life of your teen, it may also be important for her to work with a mental health professional so that she can learn skills for managing her emotions in safer and healthier ways. It's not necessary for her to delve into why she feels as she does; she mostly needs to learn new strategies for managing her emotions skillfully. When she's able to manage her internal struggles more effectively, she may be better able to follow medical advice and/or eat and behave in healthier ways.

Diane's parents may (1) return to the doctor who treated her for her foot injury so that the doctor can reinforce that continued running may create more long-term problems and (2) check with Diane's pediatrician to see whether her weight and blood work are within normal limits. The doctor can also assess the level of the problem and help Diane and her parents decide whether she also needs to work with a nutritionist or, perhaps, with a mental health professional. These professionals can also educate Diane about the impact of poor nutrition on health, thinking, and judgment. A mental health professional might help Diane recognize the emotions that might be leading to these problems and help her manage these emotions in healthier ways.

Balanced Parent Responses

If you're the parent of a teen who has disordered eating behaviors, you're faced with the apparent contradiction of wanting to guide your teen to eat healthily *and* not getting into power struggles that may cause her to be more controlling about her eating behaviors. You may wonder how to balance keeping your teen healthy, which you see as your role, and letting go of the battle over food, which you may see as giving up. Let's look at the positive and negative consequences of pushing your teen versus letting go of trying to control the eating issue:

Pushing Your Teen to Eat Healthily

Positive Consequences

- There's a chance she *may* eat better and be healthier.

- You'll feel, in the moment, like you're taking active steps to improve the situation.

Negative Consequences

- There might be an increase in anger, irritability, or power struggles.

- She may become more rigid and eat less because she feels she's being controlled.

- Relationships in the family may continue to deteriorate.

Letting Go of Your Involvement in Getting Your Teen to Eat

Positive Consequences

- You and she may be less angry at each other.

- There will be fewer power struggles that have an impact on the whole family.

- Home life may be less outwardly tense.

- She may feel more empowered and in control, and she may use her other skills or the feedback from professionals.

- She may eventually begin to eat in a healthier manner.

Negative Consequences

- You may continue to feel helpless and powerless.

- You may feel that you have given up and are not meeting your responsibility as a parent.

- You may feel more anxiety.

- Your teen may feel as if you no longer care.

- Your teen may not make any changes to her behaviors.

The most effective response is a balanced approach in which you provide structure for healthy eating in your home—which may include eating dinner together as a family, keeping healthy food available, and minimizing junk food in the house—and recognize that you cannot control the choices and decisions that your teen makes. When you create a family meal each day, or several days a week, it doesn't mean that your teen will join you. It does mean that she will witness typical and healthy eating habits and perhaps choose to join you sometime in the future. A balanced approach—one in which you both accept what you cannot change *and* provide opportunities for change—will be most effective, and lessen the tension that might have taken over your home.

If you're parenting a teen who has anorexia, food may well become the focus of your attention per the guidelines of the professionals you're working with. It's important that you follow their treatment plans as consistently as possible. If you aren't parenting a teen with anorexia, it's important that you not make food and eating the main focus of all of your attention and that you balance helping your teen develop healthy attitudes toward food with also letting your teen have some control over her life. When food becomes the focus in a family and parents are constantly attending to the teen's eating habits, emotions tend to escalate, resulting in anger, frustration, and sometimes aggression. You will need to maintain a healthy balance in your own emotions over this issue.

Diane's parents might balance their responses in several ways. They may help Diane find an exercise that meets her needs without causing more damage while helping her to accept that exercise can be done in moderation. They can talk to her about what healthy foods they'll keep in the house that she may find satisfying and also develop a family dinner several times a week with foods that Diane agrees to eat. Diane's parents can also find a more effective way of responding to Diane by *not* focusing their attention on her exercising or food intake.

Using Consequences Effectively

You may wonder how you can use reinforcement and negative consequences to change your teen's behavior around food. Will it be effective for you to (1) reinforce healthy eating or link earning privileges to it, (2) lock up foods if your teen is bingeing, (3) lock the bathroom doors after every meal if your teen is purging, (4) sit with your teen while she's eating and not let her leave the table until she does, or (5) search her room for evidence of food and examine the bathroom for evidence of vomit? How do you minimize struggles and also support and reinforce healthy eating?

Teens who have intense and overwhelming emotions often react intensely when they're embarrassed or ashamed of their behaviors, as is usually the case with disordered eating. Therefore, a constant focus on food and eating and threatening your teen with a loss of privileges for engaging in disordered eating frequently result in increased tension, distress, and struggles within the family. Discussing food-related issues may sometimes result in violent emotional outbursts. If your teen is under the treatment of specialists, the hope is that she will follow the guidelines established by those professionals. At the same time, you'll benefit from being mindful of the situations that trigger outbursts from your teen (such as commenting on food, encouraging her to behave in a healthier way, noting how she looks) so that they can be minimized.

As is the case with any self-harming behavior that results from intense emotions, it is difficult to reinforce or punish the behavior. Punishing the behavior is particularly ineffective because it focuses so much attention on a negative behavior and usually does not result in a change. The aim is to replace the behavior with healthier alternatives and to reinforce those alternatives. For example, your teen may receive extra privileges for having dinner with the family and, if she is purging, for spending an hour with the family after she finishes eating. Eating healthy snacks or following the nutritionist's advice may mean that she is able to do an activity that she likes or is really looking forward to. In all of these situations, it's important that you do not constantly remind her to eat with the family or stay away from the bathroom; the behavioral expectations should be set up in advance so that she knows what's expected and so privileges are granted if the behavior is completed.

At the same time, be particularly attuned to the behaviors of your teen if she's purging and be aware of time spent in the bathroom, especially after eating. While this is problematic behavior, it is best responded to with a nonemotional acknowledgment of the facts ("I know that you just purged") and an encouraging statement about hope for the future ("We're working on helping you get better so that you can be healthy"). If your teen is in treatment, instances of purging can be shared with the medical or mental health professional so that they can be addressed.

If your teen binges and eats food that is meant for the rest of the family, you may have to resort to locking cabinets and only allowing her access to some of the food. This may feel extreme for the family, although it's a natural consequence; when your teen is unable to control some behaviors, external controls may be necessary until she is able to develop internal controls to manage her impulse to eat.

Your main focus is to reinforce with attention those instances when your teen behaves in safe and healthy ways—when she (1) eats in a healthy way rather than restricting, (2) eats in moderation rather than overeating, (3) exercises in moderation, and/or (4) stays away from the bathroom if purging is an issue. In these situations, you can use the warmth of your relationship with your teen and parental praise to acknowledge the efforts she's making to change her eating and food habits.

Teens and Food Logs

In some treatments, your teen may be asked to complete a food log as part of her treatment for disordered eating behavior. You might want to see what's written in the log or remind her to complete it. But this may actually cause her to be less cooperative and might, inadvertently, interfere with treatment. She may hesitate to be honest about her eating habits if she knows you will be looking at the log, so it's best if you leave it to your teen and the professional who asked for it to be completed. If, at any time, your teen chooses to share her log with you, she's providing you with an opportunity to praise her work.

Acceptance

You may have a very hard time accepting behaviors that have such detrimental short- and long-term effects on the health of your teen. It's important to remember that you're not accepting the behavior—you're accepting that your teen is trying to manage painful and difficult emotions and needs to learn healthy ways to do this. Once it develops, disordered eating behavior is very difficult to manage and change, and your teen may spend many years reversing what has become familiar and comforting behavior. Teens who have disordered eating behavior struggle to find ways to control their internal chaos as well as manage the shame and guilt of the behavior itself.

Reminding yourself that your teen is doing the best she can, while also remembering that she will have to try harder to change these behaviors, will help you to accept your teen, although not her behaviors. She does need to know that you believe in her capabilities and understand her pain. It's only through knowing that you will stand by her, that you will continue to fight for her, and that you will always love her that she'll be able to engage in the very arduous work of changing her behaviors.

Summary

If your teen has disordered eating behaviors, you will parent most effectively when you can manage your anxiety over the health of your teen and avoid, as often as possible, engaging in power struggles around food. It will help you to remember that your teen struggles with painful emotions and that she will benefit from your validation even as you continue to foster healthy eating in your home.

Key Points:

- Your teen who has disordered eating behaviors is managing internal pain and chaos, despite often appearing competent and in control outwardly.

- You will benefit from getting feedback and guidance from a medical team who continually assesses the health of your teen.

- You will be most effective when you balance providing a structure for healthy eating with recognizing that you cannot control your teen's behavior.

- You will be most helpful if you reinforce healthy eating behaviors while avoiding ongoing struggles over disordered eating.

Part 3

Caring for Self and Family

Chapter 9

Self-Care for Parents

Parenting adolescents is difficult as they navigate the task of developing identities separate from their parents while parents also wrestle with holding on and letting go. The pull and tug between a teen's desire to become independent along with his very real dependency and need for structure and support both affects and is affected by a parent's desire to provide guidance and safety. There is a great deal of support for those parents whose teens are going through the typical parent-adolescent struggles. As the parent of a teen who has intense emotions, however, you may feel as though others don't understand the intensity of the emotional roller coaster you experience; that others cannot possibly comprehend what it's like to live every day with the worry that your teen may become violent or that every conversation can result in a verbally abusive outburst; that others cannot possibly know what it's like to live with the fear that your teen might harm or kill himself. You may feel isolated, alone, embarrassed, and weary. When you begin to share your struggles, you'll find that you actually have a lot of company in parents who wrestle with similar situations and feelings. You're not alone if you recognize any of these situations and emotions:

- living in a constant, heightened state of anxiety, fear, anger, and/ or frustration

- feeling blamed by others and embarrassed by, or angry about, others' reactions to you

- experiencing tension and disagreement with your partner about how to parent

- experiencing stress-related physical ailments

- experiencing the effect of the financial sacrifices caused by seeking ongoing effective treatment

- feeling frustrated if treatment has not resolved the problems over time

- feeling guilty that you might have caused or contributed to your teen's problems

- reacting to your teen's negative comments about you by questioning yourself and your parenting

- living with the frustration that you cannot fix the problems your teen experiences

- being unable to enjoy aspects of your life because of your teen's problems and pain

- living with fears for your teen's future

In this chapter, we'll discuss how you can (and need to) meet your own needs while you're parenting a teen or young adult who has intense emotions. We'll discuss several skills that can be effective in helping you reduce your own emotional vulnerability, soothe your intense emotions, and find ways to enjoy your life. Remember that the only way that you'll have the energy and resources to help your teen is if you take care of yourself. It's also important to remember that you do deserve pleasure in your life.

Living with a Teen Who Has Intense Emotions

If your child has always struggled with emotional vulnerability and high emotional sensitivity, by the time he becomes a teen, you're probably exhausted and emotionally vulnerable yourself. Moving with your teen through the typical tasks of adolescence with the added complication of emotional intensity is incredibly challenging. If typical teens are moody and sometimes distant or angry at their parents, teens who have intense emotions may be depressed, suicidal, self-harming, or anxious to the point of feeling paralyzed. Your teen may respond to what in other families are typical parent requests or limits with such verbal or physical abuse and aggression that outsiders may be needed to settle down the situation.

Parenting a child and then a teen who has intense emotions may cause conflict within your marriage or between you and your coparent. You may often disagree about the most effective way to respond to your teen, with one of you sometimes wanting to dismiss the difficulties as typical while the other may recognize problems sooner. Or one of you may feel that the way to parent is to allow independence so that your teen can learn from his mistakes, while the other parent thinks it's more effective, and less worrisome, to be protective and controlling in an attempt to lessen risk. You may feel blamed and inadequate. When your child has been in various forms of therapy, sometimes for years, the financial and time considerations create significant additional stress.

Remembering that there can be validity in multiple perspectives and that there is no one right or one wrong way to parent might lessen some tensions between you and your coparent as you look for a middle path that will help you to effectively parent together. It's very important to resist any attempt to blame yourself or others for your teen's problems. Focus instead on sensitivity and acceptance—and searching for the most effective way to move forward.

Some parents give up their jobs to be full-time caregivers and advocates for their teen. In this, they may have given up opportunities for distraction from the upheaval in their homes and they lose opportunities to feel competent and capable. Other parents try to balance their own professional lives with the need to keep their teen safe, perhaps struggling to get him to school or work or to attend school meetings or appointments when problems develop, or coming home after work to the emotional intensity and needs of the teen. Finding a balance in meeting your own needs and his may feel impossible. You may constantly feel like you're not doing an effective job either at work (where you may be interrupted by desperate phone calls from your teen or the school) or at home (where you may not know how to handle the chaos, even though you can handle difficulties at work).

Well-meaning teachers, neighbors, and friends may offer advice without realizing the extent of the effect of intense emotions, or may talk about their own successful experiences and strategies with very different children. Discussions with others who may not understand the issues may leave you exhausted as well as feeling blamed and even more isolated. You may continue to mourn the child you wish you had, or see yourself as an inadequate or incompetent parent when you listen to stories about how effective other parents can be.

Furthermore, as you advocate for your teen to get the most effective treatment or try to help others be more understanding or validating, you may find yourself at odds with, or blamed by, insurance companies, mental health facilities or practitioners, schools, or hospitals. And then your teen may not access the services you've tried so hard to find for him—or his progress with these services may be much slower than you had hoped. Some days you may be able to remember that your teen is doing the best he can; on other days, you may be too overwhelmed or frustrated to be patient or understanding. At different times, you may feel sad, disappointed, angry, confused, and/or overwhelmingly frustrated. It may feel like stress is an everyday visitor in your life, and the only variable is *how much* stress you feel at any given moment. The importance of taking care of yourself cannot be minimized. You must learn how to be kind to yourself despite forces that seem to make this incredibly difficult. When you take care of yourself, you'll be better able to wisely and effectively parent your teen in the face of his intense emotions.

Skills and Strategies for Your Well-Being

You'll find that many of the strategies and skills we have previously discussed as useful for your teen will also help you manage your own painful emotions. You may find it easier to apply strategies to your parenting than to your own emotions and needs, and you may try to "stuff your feelings"—that is, deny them or otherwise ignore them—as you take care of the needs of your teen. And yet feelings cannot be successfully ignored or dismissed; accepting your feelings and responding to them effectively will help you and your whole family.

Responding to Judgments

You may have the experience that as you talk to others about the needs of your teen, they judge, blame, or invalidate *you*. This can be confusing and infuriating. It's very important to remember that *you are doing, and have done, the best you can under difficult circumstances.* In order to let go of these negative judgments from others, you can practice saying statements like these:

- "Others don't know what my life is like, and I have a right to my own thoughts and feelings."

- "I don't have to accept someone else's judgment or feel guilty."

- "I can't change others, despite my attempts to help them understand."

- "I *can* choose how to respond to what they're saying and to let go of their judgments."

Get support from those who understand, who show you sensitivity and empathy, and keep your distance from those who don't. It's as important for *you* to be self-protective as it is for you to protect your teen from those who don't understand.

Just as you're learning to be less judgmental of your teen and to let go of judgments from others, it's also very important to become less judgmental of yourself. Judgments, even self-judgments, not only make you feel worse, but they also make it harder for you to think wisely and effectively. Consider these suggestions on how to become more accepting and less judgmental of yourself:

- Avoid negatively evaluating your own behaviors.

- Try to let go of what you *should do* and focus on what's most effective.

- Accept your own emotions, even those that are uncomfortable.

- Allow yourself to compassionately accept your own imperfections or mistakes.

As you become more adept at applying these concepts to your own behavior, you'll find that you feel better. It will also be easier to see your teen's behaviors with a wider lens and respond more effectively.

Validating Yourself

You have learned that accepting that your teen is doing the best he can, given the circumstances of his life, and parenting accordingly, will help to lessen the intensity of his emotions and make him more amenable to change. The same is true for you. While it's not unusual to be judgmental and invalidating of yourself, even as you're becoming less so of your teen, remember that you're living a difficult life that isn't your fault and that you're doing the best you can, *even when you make mistakes.*

Parent Practice: Validating Yourself

- Acknowledge that your emotions make sense, given your life circumstances.

- Notice judgments and let them pass, as you recognize and acknowledge that they're not useful.

- Be kind to yourself and accept your emotions.

- Accept yourself.

Mindfulness practice helps you become aware of your thoughts and feelings and become more accepting of yourself. Try this one simple mindfulness exercise now:

Mindfulness for Parents

Set a timer for two minutes. Find a breathing pattern that's comfortable. When you inhale, say to yourself, *Mindfully breathing.* When you exhale, say to yourself, *Letting go of judgments* or simply *Letting go.* Feel the calm as you let go of self-judgments and breathe in self-acceptance.

Balancing Demands and Wants

From the day a child is born, parents constantly seek a balance between the responsibilities and expectations that come with caring for their children (no matter what age) and their own desires and wants. These questions may sound familiar to you:

- "Can I leave my teen alone to complete his homework or chores so that I can go to the gym or take a walk?"

- "Can I meet a friend if my teen is upset and there's a possibility that he may want to talk to me about why he's so upset?"

- "Can I go away for the weekend when I'm worried about my teen's safety, even if I've taken all the precautions and provided all the supervision necessary?"

- "Is it okay for me to do some of the activities I enjoy when my teen is hurting?"

How do you balance demands (what others expect of or want from you) and wants (those things that are important to you)? Which do you give the greater weight? Think about what others demand from you and what you want. It's easy to see that the more you meet others' demands, the less time you have for yourself, and the more you do what you want, the less you may be able to do for others.

Only you can decide how to balance wants and demands in a way that feels comfortable to you. You know that meeting all of your needs all the time and not attending to the needs of others is neither effective nor responsible; and while it might sound wonderful to think about just taking care of yourself, you know you won't feel good about yourself if you do. You also know that not meeting any of your needs while meeting the needs of others will leave you depleted, frustrated, and resentful. You, like all parents in your circumstance, need to find a balance in which you meet some of your own needs while fulfilling your responsibilities to others. The key to discovering where this balance lies is in how you feel (not in how others judge you); if you feel resentful and angry, spend more time doing what you want by increasing pleasant activities in your life. If you feel as if you're not meeting your responsibilities, give more weight to the needs of others. If you feel comfortable with what you do, and feel as though you meet your own needs *and* your responsibilities, then your life is balanced in a way that works for you.

Taking Care of Yourself

You may be more vulnerable to negative emotional reactions or more easily triggered when you're tired, hungry, not feeling well physically, or are facing a particularly stressful day. You may also be more vulnerable when you're depleted of emotional energy or when you haven't taken the time to be kind to yourself. When you're parenting a teen who has intense emotions, it's especially important to make sure you exercise, sleep well, eat healthy meals, and so on. It's equally important that you build activities into your life, when possible, that you enjoy. Make sure you spend time with friends who are supportive and validating, or take time for quiet and solitude. Do those activities that will help you recharge and refresh; they will give you the energy and fortitude to respond to your teen most effectively.

Tolerating Stress Skillfully

Teach yourself to calm down and distract or soothe yourself in difficult or painful circumstances so that you can reduce the intensity of your emotions and get through the moment without making it worse (Linehan 1993b). Despite your instinctive desire to sacrifice your own pleasurable activities in order to take care of your teen and meet his needs, it's critically important to make time to take care of yourself because you're important *and* so that you have the energy to parent most effectively. At a moment of crisis, some of these skills can help you remain calm so that you can problem-solve despite the emotional turmoil that may surround you.

When your teen yells or expresses anger intensely, it often *feels* better in the moment to yell back, become defensive, or increase your demands of him to be respectful of you. However, these emotional reactions may worsen your teen's negative mood (and behaviors) and will most likely make you feel worse about yourself. Find activities that can help you respond wisely in moments of turmoil. Take a minute for mindfulness (focus on your breath, using the mindfulness practice that was discussed earlier in the chapter).

Parent Practice: Building Pleasant and Relaxing Activities into My Life

Take a piece of paper and write down a list of activities that help you feel calm. (Use the list below for ideas.) Share your list with a partner or friend who can remind you, if necessary, how to take care of yourself.

To calm yourself in a crisis, you might:

- Go for a walk or a jog.

- Take time out for quiet away from the situation.

- Take a momentary mental vacation somewhere calm and peaceful.

- Focus on something around you that brings you calm (such as a picture or painting).

- Use nice-smelling lotion (strategically placed in your home) by rubbing it gently into your hands.

- Rinse your face with cold water.

- Interact with your pet.

- Eat or drink something soothing.

- Listen to calming music.

- Talk to a friend who can listen or provide validation.

While these strategies help lower your emotional intensity in the moment, also consider adding other activities into your life to help build resiliency and increase your tolerance for stress in the long run. You may find adding activities like these into your life helpful:

- reading

- doing puzzles

- getting a massage

- gardening

- exercising regularly

- engaging in prayer or other spiritual activities

- engaging in hobbies that you enjoy

- going to dinner with friends

- helping others

- watching funny movies or television programs

Observing Your Limits

A good way to ensure that your life is balanced is to recognize, acknowledge, express, and observe your own limits. Everyone has limits, and when we have pushed ourselves or been pushed too far, we feel exhausted and drained and have no energy to do anything, let alone parent effectively. You may want to set a limit when someone asks you to do a task when you are tired and just want to take time for yourself, or if someone calls or wants to talk to you late at night when you are ready to go to sleep. You might want to say no to a request that you make something different for your teen when you have already made a nice dinner for everyone else. Be aware of your needs and establish your limits wisely. Say no when you want to or yes only when it will not stress you excessively. Accept that your limits are unique to you; don't judge yourself for your limits or accept the judgments of others (including your teen). When you're able to observe your own limits and express them respectfully to others, you'll be able to communicate and parent more effectively.

Teens often test your limits and you may try to stretch them; in these situations, the resulting communication can lead to an emotional outburst from you, your teen, or both. Though your teen may accuse you of not caring, there's no need to defend yourself. If you allow your teen to consistently breach your limits, you'll be communicating through your behavior that it's okay for him to continue to try to do so. The outcome of this is usually not positive. *It's up to you to observe your own limits, follow through, and be consistent.* Outline your limits calmly in advance and remind your teen of them in the moment so that communication and interactions can be more effective, and pleasant, in both the short and the long run. Here's an example of observing limits:

> *You know that you're exhausted by 10:00 p.m. and are therefore not able to think clearly or wisely. Trying to communicate with your teen after this hour will usually not be effective and may lead to an interaction that's negative for both of you. If your teen knows that you won't help with homework late at night, you'll want to remind him of that when he asks for help at 10:30. Don't get caught up in the*

moment and try to do the homework or explain things to him then. You'll recognize what he does not—that helping then won't work well. While it isn't easy to send your teen away and miss the opportunity to help him with his homework, especially when he doesn't reach out very often, it's still important to do so. At the same time, remember to acknowledge his disappointment and tell him that you will welcome the opportunity to help him in the morning, even very early, when you are more awake and alert.

Acceptance

You know that your life is difficult and that your teen presents you with problems and difficulties that you never anticipated. You and your teen may not be able to change this fact. If you try to deny this, dismiss it, ignore it, or make it go away, you'll remain stuck in a miserable state. When you accept the realities of your life, you'll find that what you *can* change is how you respond to your circumstances. Paradoxically, acceptance brings a sense of calm. And what you can balance is an acceptance that life is more painful and difficult than you expected with the hope that life will be better in the future. Acceptance doesn't mean giving in or giving up. It doesn't mean that you're resigned to a life of misery. Quite to the contrary, it means that you recognize the problem at hand and that you can now problem-solve so you can make the future better.

Before you recognized that your teen had intense emotions, you weren't able to get him the help he needed. You stayed stuck in a situation that didn't get better. Once you were able to accept that your teen had problems, you were able to begin the process of helping him more effectively. Acceptance is necessary for change. While accepting that your teen has problems doesn't mean that you can change him, it does mean that you can begin to change the environment so that he has the opportunity to change. You have not given up; you have enabled yourself and your teen to move forward.

Acceptance is an active process. It requires (1) being aware of the moment, (2) being open to new perspectives, (3) relaxing your body, (4) being willing to acknowledge painful realities, and (5) turning your mind to new ideas and new interpretations (Linehan 1993b). It means letting go of what you thought and what you wished and acknowledging what you have. The present reality may not be what you wanted *and it is what it is.* Accepting gives you the possibility of creating a better future.

Your teen may always have intense emotions and life might continue to be difficult for him and for you. You may despair that life will always be a struggle. Some teens and young adults will be able to manage their emotions more safely and skillfully over time as they mature, as their brains develop and as they learn how to think through their actions with a focus on long-term results. Other teens will benefit from professional help that teaches them how to live the life they want through the use of healthy and adaptive behaviors. Still other teens will continue to fight those around them who encourage the use of healthier behaviors. In some cases, the difficulties—and your stress, disappointment, and frustration—do continue into adulthood. You are on a journey, and you may not always know where you will wind up. It's important to accept this uncertainty.

It can be very hard to accept, and sometimes you have to work on accepting over and over again. Your circumstances may change, and you may have to work on accepting new and possibly more distressing circumstances. You may not want to accept, and at the same time, you have no choice. *It is what it is*—and how are you going to help yourself live with a reality that you would rather not have? *Take a deep breath, allow yourself to open your eyes to see what you may not want to see; feel the pain that you would like to deny, talk about it, and know that accepting it is a path forward on a very difficult journey.* You can have a life that you enjoy, a life that is rich and fulfilling even if there is and may always be some pain caused by the difficulties of your teen or young adult.

Acceptance is the path to change for your teen and for you. Remember that your teen is doing the best he can—and so are you.

Summary

In this chapter, we described the challenges you face as a parent whose teen has intense emotions. We discussed how hard it is to live in a state of constant stress and turmoil and the ways that you can help yourself in these situations.

Key Points:

- It's important not to judge yourself or accept the judgments of others.

- You can find ways to distract and soothe yourself and enjoy pleasurable activities.

- In order to parent effectively, observe your own limits and balance taking care of others with taking care of yourself.

- The path to change is through accepting the reality of the life you have.

Chapter 10

Siblings and Extended Family Members

As a parent of a teen or young adult who has intense emotions and behaviors, your life may be consumed by managing crises and taking care of her. It's hard to think about the other family members whose lives are also affected by the turmoil and intense emotionality in your home. It may also be hard to understand the feelings of more distant relatives who may not live with you and love your teen nonetheless. You might feel so overwhelmed by the questions you receive and the challenges you face that you may feel too depleted to validate the feelings, or meet the needs, of siblings or other family members.

Other children in your family bear witness, sometimes in silence, to the same behaviors that have overwhelmed, frustrated, or scared you. The worry and stress that is constant for you may be present for everyone else who lives with or loves your teen. Siblings may experience some or all of these thoughts and emotions:

- confusion about behaviors that they don't understand

- fear, worry, or anxiety

- desperation to help and not knowing if, or how, they can

- experiencing themselves as "invisible" if their needs or feelings are not acknowledged

- a valid recognition that you may not be able to meet their needs, which leads them to hide their worries and concerns so as not to burden you

- a desire to protect you by acting fine and as if they're managing their lives without difficulty

- a feeling that the only way to get their needs met, or to get any attention, is to act in ways similar to their sibling

Other relatives may also be confused by the behavior of your teen, and their lack of understanding and the way they respond to you may lead you to feel blamed or judged. You may feel too ashamed to share the totality of your life experience, which further alienates them from you. You may miss the support you desperately need when relatives tell you what to do without the insight needed to be truly helpful. You may feel the desire to further isolate yourself from the people who, in other circumstances, might be helpful.

When your teen has emotional difficulties, others in your extended family don't know what to do and may even keep their distance, thinking (usually erroneously) that you desire privacy. They don't bring the casserole, help with your other children, or provide the assistance that they might if your child had a physical illness. Your emotional distress, as well as the emotional distress of the other children in your family, may be exacerbated by this isolation.

Complicating this may be the desire of your teen to maintain privacy and your willingness to maintain her confidentiality. Your teen may not want others, even her siblings, to understand the level of her problems. She may react emotionally to hearing you talk to her siblings or other family members about her or about how you feel. You may hesitate to reach out for support in order to preserve your teen's privacy.

It's understandable that you may feel too exhausted to address the feelings of other family members. And you also recognize that your other children need you as well. They, too, are working through the tasks of growing up, and they're trying to manage their lives amid the upheaval in the home. As you acknowledge the needs and feelings of siblings or other relatives, don't feel more guilt. Remember that you have been doing, and continue to do, the best you can under very difficult and painful circumstances.

In this chapter, we'll discuss the feelings and needs of siblings and how you can address them, despite all the challenges you're facing. We'll also discuss how to respond to your other relatives in ways that may prove beneficial to you and them.

Siblings

The sisters and brothers of your teen who has intense emotions live with the same emotional outbursts, turmoil, stress, aggression, or fears that you live with. At home, they may live with verbal or physical abuse (directed at them or that they witness directed at you). They experience emotional fear for the safety of their sister or brother (and sometimes for you or themselves), are confused about erratic and inconsistent behaviors ("Today she seems like my normal sister; yesterday she was out of control"), and may despair for the family. They are, however, often not directly involved in the situation, might be left in the dark as to what's happening and why, and are even more powerless to be helpful in any way. Unbeknownst to you, your pain may be shared by them. They often worry about you.

The experience, and your responses, may be different depending on the age of the siblings and their birth order. Younger siblings, who might be understandably afraid, might need to be sheltered and protected as much as possible; your explanations to them might be very simple (such as "Your sister is feeling very angry and upset today"). Older siblings might feel like they should be more involved in helping their sibling or you; you may have to limit their sense of responsibility and explain things more fully ("I know you're worried about your brother's self-harm and there isn't anything you can do to help him right now"). Likewise, your reactions and responses and those of the sibling may differ depending on whether the sibling is older or younger than his sister or brother who has intense emotions. Despite these differences, your response to all siblings will be to listen, to hear and validate their feelings, and to be available to talk or spend time with them when you're able to do so. Siblings need you, too. And they need to be encouraged to pursue their own interests, their own activities, and their own friends. You can help them continue to live their own lives in the fullest possible way while also recognizing the difficulties they face.

Validation

Siblings, like their parents, need to know that what they're thinking and feeling makes sense given their experiences. Imagine how difficult it would be to feel jealous of all the attention a sibling receives when she's in the hospital. Or to be really angry at a sister or brother who has been described as "ill" and should perhaps be getting sympathy instead. Hearing that they're entitled to whatever they feel can be overwhelmingly reassuring to siblings of any age, especially when they aren't sure what they "should" be feeling or what's right or wrong. While acknowledging the difficult emotions of your other child(ren) might be very painful and difficult for you, you can understand why it's just as necessary to the emotional health of the siblings to be heard and validated as it is for your teen who has intense emotions.

Understanding the Feelings and Needs of Older Siblings

Siblings who may themselves be teens in high school or beyond are old enough to be very aware of the turmoil in the home and the way it's disrupting their lives. They may believe that their sister or brother is acting out to get their parents' attention or just using destructive means to get whatever she wants. They may be angry at you for "giving in." If their sibling is younger than them, they can see that their sibling's life is very different from the one they are experiencing and may feel guilt about any satisfaction they feel in their own lives. If their sibling is older than they are, they may worry about what their own future might look like. They may have always lived in fear or worry.

Older siblings may experience feelings like these:

- anger that their sibling is so negatively affecting their family life and you

- fear that their sibling might die, or harm herself or someone else

- embarrassment when police are called or their family's difficulties are made public

- guilt if they're enjoying their lives when their sibling is in such distress, or when they need your attention and feel their sibling needs it more

- bittersweetness as they accomplish and achieve while knowing that their sibling might not have these experiences

- confusion about if and how they can be helpful to you or their sibling who has intense emotions

- anger or disappointment when you may be unavailable to them or unresponsive to their needs

- isolated by their shame and unwillingness to share their family problems with others

- angry and afraid when abusive behavior is aimed at them

- disappointed in themselves if their needs become apparent to you, or if they feel they have not met their own expectations to be perfectly responsible for themselves

- responsibility for making things right and disappointment when they're not able to

- sadness at not having the kind of relationship with their sibling that they had hoped to have

- anger about unfairness as they witness that their sibling may not be expected to do what they are

- afraid that they'll have to take care of their sibling when they're older

You might find yourself wanting to solicit the help of an older sibling in monitoring or engaging his sister or brother who has intense emotions. You might have the urge to enlist his help by asking if he's seen razors in the bathroom or heard anything about self-harm or substance use, or asking him to include his withdrawn or isolated sibling in activities. At the same time, the sibling might be feeling responsible for keeping his sister or brother safe or for maintaining confidences. He might want to be his sibling's confidant while also providing support to you. This is quite a dilemma. It's important not to put the healthier sibling in the middle or ask him to, in any way, monitor or be responsible for his sister or brother. This would be a burden for him to carry and an overwhelming responsibility, even if you don't hear these complaints or even if he asks to be involved. Your healthier child needs to be given permission by you to have his own life and activities and to enjoy them without guilt. His responsibility begins and ends with notifying you or another adult if he's aware of the possibility of danger or harm. It's up to you to recognize the full array of confusing and painful emotions he feels and to help him live his life at the same time.

Validating the Feelings of an Older Sibling

You may find yourself frustrated that an older sibling doesn't understand the problems of his sister or brother when he makes demands or expresses his anger or frustration. It may feel as though you can't address one more source of negativity, and you may become angry at him for being insensitive to you and his sibling. When you're overwhelmed, it's hard to remember what others are experiencing. Or you may be aware of what your other children are going through, and you may worry that they express so few needs of their own. It's important for you to be aware of your own feelings so that you can address them; it's also necessary for you to be able to think wisely so that you can provide the validation that an older sibling needs.

One of the ways that you can acknowledge the feelings and needs of your other children is by spending time with them. Giving your full attention to healthier siblings is one way to say that you understand all they're going through and that you're there for them. This alone can be healing.

Here are some other ways to validate an older sibling by verbally acknowledging what's real to him:

- "It's hard to be living in this house right now. It must feel awful to you."

- "Of course you're embarrassed when the police come to our house."

- "I'm sure others would get as angry as you if their sister or brother treated them that way."

- "I know you're scared that something bad might happen. I share this fear with you."

- "I get that you want to do something to help. It must be so frustrating for you when you can't, just as it is for me."

- "It must be so difficult when I don't always have the time for you that I wish I had."

- "I know it feels unfair to you when you think we treat your sibling differently."

In the midst of an incident with your teen who has intense emotions, you may not be able to be validating or understanding of her sibling. After things have calmed down, it's important to go to him, listen if he wants to talk, and if he doesn't, respect his desire not to talk. Remember to acknowledge his feelings. This will help the older sibling know that he's important, too, and that you care, that you accept him and his feelings, and that you understand. This response from you will also enable him to accept that you're doing the best you can to meet his needs. Having this knowledge is invaluable to his own healthy development.

Older siblings also need to know that they have your permission to enjoy themselves and take care of their own needs, and that they don't have to feel responsible for their brother or sister. They're allowed to find ways to distract themselves or soothe themselves in those moments of intense emotionality at home. For example, they can use headphones so that they don't have to listen to angry voices or verbal attacks. They can take a shower to soothe and distract themselves; or they can take their pet, if they have one, for a walk or into their room. And you can make sure that they participate in activities they enjoy and find ways to feel competent and accomplished.

Understanding the Feelings and Needs of Younger Siblings

Younger siblings—who may be preteens or even younger—may be very afraid and confused about what they see or experience in their home. Emotional outbursts, verbal or physical abuse, or aggression will understandably scare a younger child, who may no longer feel that his home is a safe place and may not understand why his parents are so angry or so sad. If he's a little older, he may understand that his sibling is very sad or upset, and he may want to help her feel better. Those younger, healthier kids whose sister or brother is self-harming might actually see the evidence in a bathroom they share, and might not know how to help or stop the self-harm. If their sibling is older, they may feel the loss of having a big brother or sister that they can talk to. If their sibling is younger, they may feel responsible in ways that are a burden to someone their age. They may deny their own needs so that they don't further burden you. Here are some of the thoughts and feelings that younger siblings might have in common with older siblings:

- fears about their own safety

- anger that their home may be in such turmoil

- embarrassment if their family's struggles become public

- worry about what might happen to their sibling, to their family, and to them

- discomfort about sharing what they're going through with anyone else and a feeling that their peers, and even other adults, won't understand

- anger at their sibling who has intense emotions and at you, when you're not available

- confusion about how they can help

- a feeling that it's not fair that their sister or brother gets so much attention and may not have to complete chores that they have to

Validating the Feelings of Younger Siblings

Whenever possible, your younger child(ren) will benefit from your time and attention. You can listen and help them know that all of their feelings are okay and understandable. Younger siblings may also benefit from having a special adult in whom they can confide, especially when you may be consumed with your teen who has intense emotions. If possible, in the midst of emotional outbursts, it sometimes helps if one parent takes the younger child(ren) out of the house to enjoy something pleasurable as a way to both distract and soothe them. Your time and energy and willingness to hear whatever the siblings have to say will benefit them exponentially. Siblings want to know that they're important to you and that they don't have to be angry or sad to get your attention. Your responses, as much as your words, can say this to your younger children. Here are some ways that you can verbally validate younger siblings:

- "I know you're scared. Anybody would be. What can we do to help you feel better?"

- "I get that it's hard to share this stuff with your friends because you think they won't understand. Some friends will, and you can share if you want."

- "I see that you're worried about your sister. I can understand why."

- "I know it isn't fair that your brother doesn't do the chores you do."

- "You and your feelings—all of them—matter to us, too."

If there has been an incident of aggression or physical or verbal abuse in your house, your younger children will benefit if you go to them when it's over. You might find them cowering under the bed, hiding in the bathroom, or listening to music. As exhausted as you might be at these times, it's important to listen, accept, and validate your younger children's feelings in the aftermath of an incident so that they don't carry their emotions within themselves and so they can move forward with their own lives.

Providing Explanations to Siblings

Information and understanding is also helpful when managing your children's anger, sadness, and fear and reducing the worrisome behaviors that might result from these emotions. You can find ways to explain to your other children why their sibling behaves as she does, according to their age and cognitive ability. Try to provide these explanations calmly, gently, and nonjudgmentally at the same time as you listen and continue to validate the emotions of these siblings.

Siblings need to know why their brother or sister who has intense emotions behaves as she does and why you respond the way you do. Explain the biosocial theory and related issues to an older sibling:

- "Your sister's brain is wired differently from yours and the intensity of her emotions causes her to behave the way she does."

- "Your sibling's illness may not be his, or anyone else's, fault, *and* he does have to make changes so the family can get along better and he can have a better life."

- "She is more limited and overwhelmed by her intense emotions and may not be able to be as responsible with chores or homework as you are expected to be."

- "It does require a great deal of emotional energy to learn how to manage intense emotions in a safe manner, and your sibling may be working on getting well when it looks like she's doing 'nothing.'"

- "Safety is my main priority, and although it might seem as though I'm rewarding unhealthy behaviors, I am, of necessity, 'picking my battles' based on the most unsafe or dangerous behavior at the time."

- "There are times when your brother needs to withdraw from activities if he's becoming too emotional. I allow and even encourage him to do this so that he can manage his emotions less aggressively and more constructively."

Here are some things you can say to a younger sibling:

- "Your sister doesn't always behave the way we want her to. Her feelings get in the way. We're trying to help her so her behaviors won't scare everyone so much."

- "It may seem like your sister likes how she acts. She probably doesn't like it very much and would rather get along better with everyone. That's what she's working on."

- "Sometimes your brother gets very mad, madder than others ever get. He isn't mad at you; he's just mad."

- "Sometimes your sister's feelings are like a volcano and she explodes. When she does, go to your room and we'll talk when things calm down."

- "Sometimes I have to make sure that your brother doesn't hurt himself. If you ever see him hurting himself, please tell me."

- "Your brother wishes he could play with you or join the family more. It makes us all sad when he can't."

Older and younger siblings need to be helped to feel less responsible. You can tell them that, as much as they might want to, they can't make their sibling feel better—only she can do that for herself. You can remind them to share with you or another adult if they know their sibling is unsafe so they don't carry that burden alone. As hard as this is for everyone in the family to understand and accept, your teen with intense emotions has to make her own commitment to life while those who love her have the responsibility to live their own lives to the fullest extent possible.

Extended Family

You may find yourself balancing the needs and demands of your extended family (however you define it) with the needs of your teen or young adult. In direct and indirect ways, family members can be affected by the problems of your teen. They may (1) witness your distress at her behaviors, (2) witness aggression or self-harm, (3) know about psychiatric hospitalizations, or (4) feel a loss when your teen chooses not to attend family celebrations. Your relatives may not know how to respond *or* they may think they know all the answers.

You may feel tension around other family members, even if there's generally support and caring in the family. These family members may experience tension as well. You might see the success of the children of your siblings or cousins, and you may feel some embarrassment and guilt when your teen doesn't "measure up" or can't meet the spoken or imagined expectations of the family. Your teen's grandparents may expect certain behaviors, a certain level of respect, or a particular way in which family traditions are maintained. You may feel the constant tug of trying to please your parents or other relatives while also trying to be understanding and sensitive to the struggles and needs of your teen. You will find yourself seeking a balance among the needs of relatives you love, your need to be part of this family, and the needs of your teen. While you may recognize that these family members also love you and your teen, it may be very difficult for you when you experience tension around them.

Some relatives may be supportive, understanding, and validating. They may listen to your explanations and acknowledge your feelings. When you're around them, you may feel their comfort. Other relatives may appear judgmental when they see how your teen behaves and how you respond. Absent the understanding that you have of the need to develop priorities, to be validating, and to be accepting of your teen's limits, they may offer advice in attempts to be helpful. Some relatives may say you need to set firmer limits, have more consequences, or not let your teen "get away with excuses." Other relatives may think that you're not being understanding enough and that you need to let your teen find her own way. What you may feel is that, while these relatives might be trying to be helpful, their advice is anything but. You want them to understand, not tell you what to do. What you want is for someone to "get" what your life is like and understand that you're doing the best you can.

Your teen may ask you not to tell relatives about the problems she's having. This makes it difficult for you to explain why you're responding to her the way you are. You may want to respect your teen's need for privacy, while you also need relatives to understand so that you don't feel as isolated and alone. You will, under these circumstances, have to balance your need for support and understanding with your teen's need for privacy. You can understand and validate her feelings while providing enough information, without specifics or details, to the relatives who may be most supportive of and helpful to you.

You may also need to accept that some relatives, despite how much they might care about you and your teen, will not be able to understand and may continually offer unwanted or unhelpful advice. If the benefits of this relationship outweigh getting this feedback, you may choose to maintain the relationship in a way that remains meaningful to you without discussing your teen's problems and while setting limits on any advice ("I know that you're trying to be helpful. The issues are complicated, and I would prefer not to discuss them right now"). If the relationship is not a meaningful relationship, you can limit the time as well as the information that you share.

Ultimately, your main responsibility is to your teen and to yourself. You know that your teen needs your support and validation. If being with relatives is too difficult, you can let your teen make her own choices about her connections to family members and her attendance at family events. This may be difficult and painful for you, as you will feel different from the rest of your relatives and possibly celebrate family events without your teen. Acknowledge your own feelings and remember that your teen and you are doing the best you can. Continue to hope that relationships will change over time as your teen learns how to navigate interactions with others.

Providing Explanations to Relatives

Some relatives—those whom you trust to be understanding, supportive, and not judgmental—may want and benefit from having more information about the difficulties your teen faces. It might be helpful for them to know what it means to have emotional vulnerability that leads to emotion dysregulation—that is, to be born with a brain that is very sensitive to emotional situations and may lead to intense emotional responses. You can explain how this affects your whole family, and why you respond the way you do. Offer these explanations:

- The tendency to experience emotions intensely and to therefore experience the world as upsetting, painful, and destabilizing is biologically based and nobody's fault.

- It's important to be validating of your teen's feelings—although *not* of her behaviors—as a way for her to feel heard and understood. This validation and acceptance is necessary for change to occur and also leads to healthier behaviors in the family.

- Your teen's behaviors (even those that are problematic) are attempts to manage her emotions, and she needs to learn to manage them in safer and healthier ways.

- When your teen needs to take a break from a family activity, even though it can be perceived as rude or disrespectful, she is actually trying to regulate her emotions in a healthy and adaptive way.

When your relatives listen and learn from your explanations and understand what you're going through, they can be a true source of support, validation, and comfort. Their sensitivity can be invaluable, and it's important for you to accept and appreciate it.

Summary

In this chapter, we discussed the effect that your teen with intense emotions has on siblings and other members of the family. We also discussed how you can help siblings and other family members understand by explaining your teen's emotional intensity to them in a nonjudgmental and validating manner.

Key Points:

- It's important to recognize, acknowledge, and validate the feelings of your healthier children, who often feel invisible and unimportant.

- It's important to spend time with your other children and make sure their emotional needs are being met.

- Some extended family members may be helpful and supportive, while others may offer unwanted or unhelpful advice. Try to spend time with those relatives who can understand and validate your feelings and experiences.

Balanced and Effective Parenting: A Quick Guide

Below you'll find skills and concepts from the book that will help you remember how to parent in a balanced and effective way.

Be willing (to change).

Acceptance is necessary for change.

Learn new skills and strategies.

Acceptance leads to less suffering.

Note the validity in multiple points of view.

Changing behaviors is hard and necessary.

Evaluate pros and cons.

Distract temporarily from stressful situations.

and

Emotion regulation leads to behavioral control.

Find balance in your responses.

Follow through on limits and expectations.

Eliminate judgments by being mindful.

Commit to change behaviors that don't work.

Think wisely and dialectically.

Interact more effectively by knowing your goals.

Validate yourself and others.

Effective responses focus on long-term goals.

Participate with full attention.

Appreciate the moment.

Recognize and reinforce positive behaviors.

Effectiveness means doing what works.

Negotiate when necessary.

Think in a way that doesn't judge.

"It is what it is."

Natural consequences help learning and change.

Generalize skills to all situations.

Resources for Parents

Web Resources

Adolescent Mental Health Initiative—Annenberg Public Policy Center of the University of Pennsylvania

http://www.annenbergpublicpolicycenter.org/aci/adolescent-mental-health
-initiative-book-series/

Books written for and by teens with emotional difficulties

Links to other resources

Anxiety and Depression Association of America (ADAA)

http://www.ADAA.org

Resources, information, and updated research about anxiety and depressive disorders

Behavioral Tech

http://behavioraltech.org

Resources and information about dialectical behavior therapy (DBT) practitioners and about trainings from the developers of DBT

Bipolar Children

http://www.bpchildren.org

Information and newsletter for parents as well as helpful resources that can be used at home

National Alliance on Mental Illness (NAMI): Child and Adolescent Resource Center

http://www.nami.org

Information about many emotional disorders, advocacy, and education as well as parent support and psychoeducation groups

National Education Alliance for Borderline Personality Disorder (NEA-BPD)

http://www.borderlinepersonalitydisorder.com

Resources, videos, and audios about DBT, validation, and other skills

Information about Family Connections, a course that provides support and psychoeducation for parents and family members and that is facilitated by parents who are trained by professionals in the field

Treatment and Research Advancement (TARA): National Association for Personality Disorder

http://www.tara4bpd.org/dyn/index.php

Dialectical behavior therapy family workshops, resources, and information

Books for Parents

Acquainted with the Night: A Parent's Quest to Understand Depression and Bipolar Disorder in His Children by Paul Raeburn

Borderline Personality Disorder in Adolescents, 2nd Edition: What to Do When Your Teen Has BPD: A Complete Guide for Families by Blaise Aguirre

The Buddha and the Borderline: My Recovery from Borderline Personality Disorder Through Dialectical Behavior Therapy by Kiera Van Gelder

The Burden of Sympathy: How Families Cope with Mental Illness by David A. Karp

Calming the Emotional Storm: Using Dialectical Behavior Therapy Skills to Manage Your Emotions and Balance Your Life by Sheri Van Dijk

Coming to Our Senses: Healing Ourselves and the World Through Mindfulness by Jon Kabat-Zinn

Get Out of My Life, but First Could You Drive Me and Cheryl to the Mall?: A Parent's Guide to the New Teenager by Anthony E. Wolf

Loving Someone with Borderline Personality Disorder: How to Keep Out-of-Control Emotions from Destroying Your Relationship by Shari Y. Manning

Loving Someone with OCD: Help for You and Your Family by Karen J. Landsman, Kathleen M. Rupertus, and Cherry Pedrick

Madness: A Bipolar Life by Marya Hornbacher

Stop Walking on Eggshells: Taking Your Life Back When Someone You Care About Has Borderline Personality Disorder by Paul Mason and Randi Kreger

The Stop Walking on Eggshells Workbook by Randi Kreger

An Unquiet Mind: A Memoir of Moods and Madness by Kay Redfield Jamison

Wasted: A Memoir of Anorexia and Bulimia by Marya Hornbacher

Will's Choice: A Suicidal Teen, a Desperate Mother, and a Chronicle of Recovery by Gail Griffith

Books to Recommend to Teens and Young Adults

Adolescent Mental Health Initiative—Annenberg Public Policy Center of the University of Pennsylvania (books by and for adolescents about various disorders)

The Buddha and the Borderline: My Recovery from Borderline Personality Disorder Through Dialectical Behavior Therapy by Kiera Van Gelder

New Harbinger Publications (Instant Help Books for Teens—self-help books for adolescents):

The Anxiety Workbook for Teens by Lisa M. Schab

The Bipolar Workbook for Teens by Sheri Van Dijk and Karma Guindon

Don't Let Emotions Run Your Life for Teens by Sheri Van Dijk

Stopping the Pain: A Workbook for Teens Who Cut and Self-Injure by Lawrence Shapiro

The Stress Reduction Workbook for Teens by Gina Biegel

Books for Siblings

Hey! I'm Here Too: A Book for Tween/Teen Siblings of a Young Person with Emotional Issues by Pat Harvey and David Fialkoff

My Sister's Keeper: Learning to Cope with a Sibling's Mental Illness by Margaret Moorman

Apps That Provide Distractions and Soothing for Parents and Adolescents

Buddha Board – practice accepting the moment

DBT – skills and coaching

Lotus Bud – mindfulness bells and timers

Relax Melodies – soothing sounds that can be combined to create new sounds

Serenity – a mindfulness app

Transform Your Life – awareness practice

References

Fruzzetti, A. E. October 2005. *Validating and Invalidating Responses in Families.* Paper presented at Borderline Personality Disorder: Historical and Future Perspectives sponsored by NEA-BPD and McClean Hospital, Burlington, MA.

Hawton, K., and L. Harriss. 2007. "Deliberate Self-Harm in Young People: Characteristics and Subsequent Mortality in a 20-year Cohort of Patients Presenting to Hospital." *Journal of Clinical Psychiatry*, 68: 1574–83.

Linehan, M. M. 1993a. *Cognitive-Behavioral Treatment of Borderline Personality Disorder.* New York: Guilford Press.

Linehan, M. M. 1993b. *Skills Training Manual for Treating Borderline Personality Disorder.* New York: Guilford Press.

Miller, A. L., J. H. Rathus, and M. M. Linehan. 2007. *Dialectical Behavior Therapy with Suicidal Adolescents.* New York: Guilford Press.

Pat Harvey, ACSW, LCSW, has over thirty years of experience working with families, and now coaches parents and family members of youth and adults with emotion dysregulation using a dialectical behavior therapy (DBT) framework. She facilitates trainings and workshops for mental health professionals on DBT concepts, skills, and parent/family interventions throughout the United States and at national conferences. She is coauthor of *Parenting a Child Who Has Intense Emotions*, *Dialectical Behavior Therapy for At-Risk Adolescents*, and *Hey, I'm Here Too!*

Britt H. Rathbone, MSSW, LCSW, provides mental health services to adolescents and their families in the Washington, DC, area. He has decades of experience working directly with adolescents and families, is consistently voted a "top therapist" for adolescents, teaches graduate students, trains therapists, and leads a highly regarded and successful clinical practice. Rathbone lectures often on the value of using dialectical behavior therapy (DBT) and other evidence-based practices with young people. He is coauthor of *Dialectical Behavior Therapy for At-Risk Adolescents* and *What Works with Teens.*

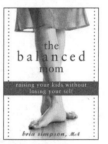